THE SILENT MAJORITY

SURVIVAL

HANDBOOK

WHAT CAN BE DONE
WHEN POLITICIANS
AND BIG GOVERNMENT
FAIL THEIR CONSTITUENTS

PETER H. WOLF

Dedication

This book is dedicated to all who have sacrificed much to defend our country's constitutionally-guaranteed freedom of pursuing happiness to the best of our abilities. I also want to dedicate this book to my parents, Lenhard and Maria Wolf, who immigrated to the United States so that my brothers and I could experience American Exceptionalism.

CONTENTS

Acknowledgement

I thank my wife, Mary, for her moral and tangible support in my humble efforts to defend liberty, including the writing of this book. I also thank Warren Edstrom, who first introduced me to the power of precinct organizing and has provided much counsel and knowledge throughout my journey to learn as much as possible about religion, sociology, economics, and politics.

Introduction

"However [political parties] may now and then answer popular ends, they are likely in the course of time and things, to become potent engines, by which cunning, ambitious, and unprincipled men will be enabled to subvert the power of the people and to usurp for themselves the reins of government, destroying afterwards the very engines which have lifted them to unjust dominion."
- **George Washington, Farewell Address, September 17, 1796**

Throughout world history, human nature has tended towards consolidation of power for a few elites at the expense of those they rule, starting with kings and queens. After monarchs were overthrown, human history gave us totalitarian regimes such as Napoleon in France, Nazis in Germany, and Communists in the Soviet Union and China. This is why the United States of America has been so unique in that the *Founding Fathers*, aware of these human tendencies, placed the power in *We the People* and attempted to prevent power consolidation in government with checks-and-balances.

Unfortunately, over time these checks-and-balances have been eroded by politicians, while a complicit press propagandizes the population to not notice the accompanying loss of power and freedom. Similarly, a complicit educational system indoctrinates our young and fails to properly teach them about the Constitution's checks-and-balances. Nobel Prize winning economist, Friedrich Hayek, captures this progression based on human nature in his 1944 book, *The Road to Serfdom*.

It is now apparent that both political parties are complicit in growing an ever more powerful federal government with an accompanying loss of freedom for the majority of people whom they should, instead, be representing. Elections in 2010, 2012, and 2014, in which the Republican Party gained majorities in both the House of Representatives and the Senate, have resulted in no reversals of this power consolidation. The only beneficiaries are the very politicians who facilitate it and the wealthy *elite* and corporate lobbyists who influence these politicians with campaign contributions and careers after politics. While one in five Americans in mid-2015 is on welfare[1], the *political elite* or *ruling class* live in the three highest per capita income counties in the country. These Washington, DC counties essentially have no industry. In essence, we have a *political elite* class that rules with absolute power over the struggling majority of people, as envisioned in George Orwell's insightful book, *1984*, written in 1948. Another excellent book which envisioned our current predicament is *It Can't Happen Here,* written in 1935 by Sinclair Lewis, who became the first writer from the United States to receive the Nobel Prize in Literature. The book is a fictional novel about *elite politicians* and big business taking over the federal government. It is ironic that the presidential candidate in this novel was elected by promising everyone $4,000, just as we were all promised $2,500 savings with Obamacare.

Our *political elite* intend to transform the United States with a change from *American Exceptionalism,* with its focus on equal opportunities, to socialism, with its focus on equal outcomes. They are attempting to accomplish this with unprecedented federal spending and debt creation in support of an ever-expanding dependency class, supported by ever-increased taxation on the productive elements of society. The result will be a redistribution of wealth. In essence, the transformation is aided by pacifying the masses with *"bread and circuses"* (handouts and diversions) and is facilitated by the *political elite's* cultural indoctrination through the media, education, and *"Social Justice"* religions. Even worse, the *political elite* are dividing those who are economically dependent on them into individual factions, each of which is fighting for its piece of the economic pie. The *Balkanization* (fragmentation or division) of Americans assures these *political elite* that no one group is large enough to overthrow them. This development is very much counter to the historical character of the United States being a *Melting Pot*.

Once this transformation is achieved, it will be nearly impossible to reverse since many constituents will have lost their motivation, self-esteem, willingness to assume risk, and skills to individually succeed. Instead, they will have adopted a mindset that "society owes them" a decent standard of life that includes housing, transportation, food, cell phones, flat-screen TVs, computers, cable and Internet access, etc.

Fortunately, constituents are waking up to this reality. The *Wall Street Journal*, in an August 27, 2015 article by Peggy Noonan, titled *"America is so in Play"*[2], cites an expert who states that, *"Over 80% of the American people, across the board, believe an elite group of political incumbents, plus big business, big media, big banks, big unions and big special interests—the whole Washington political class—have rigged the system for the wealthy and connected."* Gallup reported on September 21, 2015 that almost half of Americans, 49%, say the federal government poses *"an immediate threat to the rights and freedoms of ordinary citizens".[3]* This is in stark contrast to Gallup's polling in 2003 when only a third of the population shared this sentiment. A Fox News poll conducted in September, 2015 indicates that *"62% of Republicans Feel BETRAYED by their Party",[4]* a party that has done nothing to stop the rapidly increasing *Big Government* controlled by *political elite*, while supposedly being against it.

So what is to be done? Clearly, our participation in elections is insufficient to protect us from an ever-invasive and controlling federal government and its collaborating *elites* and media in the private sector. The *Silent Majority* must awaken and pursue proven non-violent actions as part of a liberty movement throughout communities across America. Like-minded, liberty-oriented, and Constitution-based constituents can collaborate and coordinate their actions regionally and nationally with each other through a *"Conspiracy of Ideas"* and by using social media, very much as is already done by the *ruling class.* Warren Edstrom and I co-founded *TheVoicesOfAmerica.org* in mid-2009 to benchmark the most effective methods to impact politics and policy and to make these *Get-Out-The-Vote* methods freely available nationally as a service to individuals and leaders new to the political process.

We accomplish this through our website, monthly newsletters, and on-site presentations.

Since 2009, we have traveled much and have given many presentations, including a keynote address at the first *National Tea Party Convention* in Nashville, TN in February, 2010. We met many leaders who were concerned about the direction of our country. Consistently, these leaders expressed to us that their key issues were their inability to grow their organizations and to motivate their members to action. Members would attend meetings and rallies to educate themselves and stay up-to-date, but would not sufficiently volunteer for important projects. Based on our continued, extensive research, this book will teach you many proven, effective actions that anyone can pursue to grow and motivate the *Silent Majority* and take back our country from the *political elite*. They are based on the same methods and actions used successfully by those advocating for *Big Government*. At minimum, this book explains how simply speaking up with truth and logic will be effective at exposing the *political elite*, as long as it is done with compassion and by seizing the moral high ground.

Clearly, time is of the essence! We must act now to ensure that our children and grandchildren can experience

American Exceptionalism. Otherwise, similar to the collapse of the Roman Empire, we will begin to witness the collapse of the United States and its exceptional economy and society.

To further highlight the urgency of our predicament, I encourage you to read *"they thought they were free"*, written in 1955 by Milton Mayer about Germany during the 1933-45 period. After World War II, Milton Mayer interviewed a cross-section of Germans to learn what they were thinking during the rise of totalitarianism in Germany. As the book title suggests, *"they thought they were free"*. How wrong they were!

---

[1] Rich Exner, *1 in 5 Americans receive government assistance: food stamps, welfare, Medicaid details,* Northeast Ohio Media Group, http://www.cleveland.com/datacentral/index.ssf/2015/05/1_in_5_americans_receive_gover.html (May 28, 2015).

[2] Peggy Noonan, "America Is So in Play", *Wall Street Journal*, August 27, 2015.

[3] Frank Newport, *Half in U.S. Continue to Say Gov't Is an Immediate Threat*, Gallup, http://www.gallup.com/poll/185720/half-continue-say-gov-immediate-threat.aspx (September 21, 2015).

---

[4] Jim Hoft, *SHOCK POLL: 62% of Republicans Feel BETRAYED by their Party*, Gateway Pundit, http://www.thegatewaypundit.com/2015/09/shock-poll-62-of-republicans-feel-betrayed-by-their-party-video/ (September 24, 2015).

Chapter 1

==================

The Road to Serfdom [5]

"Do not blame Caesar, blame the people of Rome who have so enthusiastically acclaimed and adored him and rejoiced in their loss of freedom and danced in his path and given him triumphal processions. Blame the people who hail him when he speaks in the Forum of the new wonderful good society which shall now be Rome's, interpreted to mean more money, more ease, more security, and more living fatly at the expense of the industrious."
- Marcus Tullius Cicero, Roman philosopher and statesman (106-43 BC)

The Nobel Prize winning economist, F. A. Hayek, in his 1944 book, *The Road to Serfdom*, wrote about how individuals lose freedoms and individual liberty as a result of ever-increasing government authority. The phases described in the book are:

- Excessive spending and debt
- Government dependency instead of jobs
- High taxation and government redistribution of wealth
- Promised equality and *Social Justice* for all
- Many government rules and regulations to achieve the utopian vision
- Government *elite politicians* collude with corporate *elite*, behaving in their own interest against the interests of the people these politicians represent
- The loss of freedom.

We are well down the path described in his book where we become serfs to *elite politicians* and their corporate benefactors and special interests. Both Republican and Democrat *Big Government* career politicians have gotten us to where we are today, i.e., an unsustainable debt and an oppressive, large government. Government's massive intrusion into the private sector reduces the *Silent Majority's* individual freedoms and liberties. Instead of incumbent politicians representing their constituents, they represent corporate lobbyists and special interests who help pay for their campaigns. In return, these politicians provide "pork" in bills as payback to their contributors. *"This unholy alliance between the largest corporations and the government is a natural and inevitable result of moving away from a national commitment to self-governance,"* wrote Scott Rasmussen in his book, *In Search of Self-Governance. "As a result, the gap today between Americans who want to govern themselves and politicians who want to rule over them may be as big as the gap between the colonies and England during the 18th century. And that's true whether Republicans or Democrats are in charge."*

While constituents suffer, *elite politicians*, corporations, and affiliated special interests prosper. This is evidenced by the booming stock market and the fact that the three highest per capita income counties in the country are in the Washington, DC area, which essentially has no industry, but is home to the government *elites*. Additional examples of how *elite politicians* take care of themselves at the expense of the *Silent Majority* are:

- *Elite politicians* in Congress and their staffers received a special dispensation under the *Affordable Healthcare Act (Obamacare)* to keep generous health subsidies, despite high incomes. Corporations received a three-year implementation delay.[6]

- During the government shutdown of 2013, the federal government went out of its way to maximize pain on individuals and small businesses while passing laws assuring back-pay to furloughed government employees, despite them not having worked during the shutdown.[7]

- During the financial crisis of 2008, GE, along with nineteen or so other large corporations, was able to extract favorable terms from lawmakers to avoid paying taxes in perpetuity using the "active financial exemption" in which income from overseas lending activities is not taxed.[8]

- While the federal government holds the private sector accountable for its actions with significant financial fines and incarceration, government bureaucrats are totally unaccountable for any of their actions or results. For example, the massive electronic theft in 2014 by hackers of all federal government employee and security-cleared contractor records occurred without substantive repercussions for government employees.

- Threats to *Big Government* are dealt with by essentially "weaponizing" government against constituents, as was observed with the IRS harassment of *limited government* Tea Party organizations before the 2012 presidential election.[9]

Elite politicians, their corporate benefactors, and special interests even prosper in difficult times, as was seen in Germany's Weimar Republic from 1919 to 1923. As described in *When Money Dies,* written by Adam Fergusson, politicians of all parties during this 1919 to 1923 period pursued deficit spending by printing money to defer having to deal with the harsh economic realities associated with the many socialist government programs and war reparation payments. This unrestrained spending is very similar to our current situation in which the Federal Reserve pursued many years of *Quantitative Easing* with near zero interest rates. The Federal Reserve essentially printed many billions of dollars and gave it to the Treasury to spend in exchange for IOU bonds. As explained in *When Money Dies*, the eventual consequence of unrestrained deficit spending is runaway inflation that destroys small businesses and the middle class. During the time of the Weimar Republic, government officials and those aligned with *Big Government*, such as big businesses, and big-labor unions, did not suffer as much as everyone else. Government employee and big-labor union salaries and wages were constantly indexed to inflation. Big businesses prospered since they inflation-indexed their product prices and pursued foreign currency exchanges to hedge against the devaluating German mark. It was the middle class and small businesses who lost everything and were wiped out!

So who is this bipartisan *elite ruling class*? *The American Spectator* had an excellent article on this matter in mid-2010 titled, *"America's Ruling Class – And the Perils of Revolution"*[10], from which key points are shared in this paragraph. Unlike the past diversity of backgrounds and thoughts, today's *ruling class* lacks diversity and shares a common belief that they are "the best and brightest", while those they rule are viewed as dysfunctional, racist, and retrograde. Most began their careers in government and leveraged their way into the private sector, based on a common language, habits, tastes, and tools of bureaucracy. The *ruling class* believes that since man evolves, man can be improved, and that they, as the most intelligent, should be the improvers. They only have the support of about one-third of the constituents they "rule", since some Democrats, most Independents, and three-fourths of voters who only reluctantly vote for Republicans do not feel they are represented by the *ruling elite*. Nevertheless, the *ruling class* machine has all the power and maintains it through patronage and promises thereof, i.e., providing tangible results to its members. Regardless of the "problems", many of which are fabricated, the central focus of solutions is on "feeding the machine" through money transfers, jobs, or privilege. Missteps or law-breaking by the *ruling class* is tolerated, while these are heavily punished if done by the *Silent Majority* opponents over whom they rule.

But how have these *elite politicians* accomplished this erosion of our federal government's checks-and-balances and amassed such centralized governmental powers to put the *Silent Majority* on this *"Road to Serfdom"*? First, the federal government uses our taxpayer monies to essentially bribe states into giving up states' rights, as protected under the Constitution's Tenth Amendment. An example is the *Common Core* educational standard which essentially federalizes education. Secondly, an unaccountable federal bureaucracy is allowed to assume powers normally reserved for the legislators. This is best exemplified by the Environmental Protection Agency "making law" with its ever-increasing control of land property, the energy sector, and industry in general. Thirdly, government gains power over constituents through its ever-expanding welfare programs, even if pursuit of this dependency requires unprecedented national debt. The increased influx of illegal immigrants since 2008, who benefit from welfare, serves this purpose. In 2013, based on Census Bureau numbers, more people were on welfare than there were year-round full-time workers.[11] Fourthly, the *political elite* just ignore the Constitution and the laws, or apply them unevenly, making us essentially a lawless society. One example is not enforcing federal immigration laws, even condoning sanctuary cities for illegal immigrants, while prosecuting and jailing those advocating for religious liberty, as guaranteed under the First Amendment of the Constitution. Other examples are: *Obamacare*, which has been illegally changed over thirty-eight times, *"Operation Choke Point"*, through which the Department of Justice and the Treasury intimidate banks to prevent them from doing business with a number of legitimate businesses, IRS' illegal selective targeting of nonprofit groups, and EPA's targeting of fossil fuel production while favoring *green energy*.

Lastly, cunning politicians advocate initiatives that are contrary to the beliefs and values of the *Silent Majority*, knowing that the only means to achieve these initiatives is through an ever-expanding federal government. *Elite politicians* are assisted in this by aligned, professional *Community Organizers* who operate invisibly behind the scenes. In 2015 alone, *Organizing for Action* plans to train an additional 10,000 *Community Organizers*[12] who are funded with hundreds of millions of dollars from *Big Government*[13]. Unfortunately, once this increased power is achieved, those for whom cunning politicians advocated these initiatives achieve little to no tangible benefits. In contrast, the *political elite* and their corporate benefactors gain wealth and power. A few observations are noted below:

- Under the government's guise of fighting racism and unequal opportunities for African-Americans; their communities' educational capabilities, employment, home ownership, community safety, and general well-being have only gotten worse.

- The *Sarbanes-Oxley* law, which passed after the 2008 recession with the intent to protect constituents from yet another recession, in essence, has allowed the federal government to take over the banking industry. The government has since used this power to essentially extort significant financial penalties for itself from banks, resulting in higher banking fees for the *Silent Majority*.

- Advocacy for a minority of uninsured resulted in a complete federal government takeover of the healthcare industry with *Obamacare*. The result has been higher healthcare-related costs for everyone, while the quality of healthcare is worse. The *ruling class* taxes its constituents with penalties, requires that all buy insurance, and thus gains absolute power by making all dependent on the "system" it controls. This healthcare law was implemented despite lies from *elite politicians* that premiums would be reduced, we could keep our insurance policies, and we could keep our doctors. As Lenin stated, *"Socialized medicine is the keystone to the arch of the Socialized State."*

- The federal government takeover of higher education student loans is leveraged by the federal government to essentially control higher education. This is because any college or university with students who receive government loans has to adhere to the government's rules and regulations. Students, in contrast, are saddled with ever- increasing debt, tuitions continue to increase well beyond inflation, and the quality of education is worse.

- The Federal Justice Department focus on white-on-black shootings, which are miniscule relative to black-on-black shootings, has the potential of federalizing police departments throughout the nation. Already, many big city police departments are being run under the supervision of the Justice Department. This has the potential of making the local police departments accountable and loyal to the federal government, instead of to the local communities.

- Immigrants are being used as votes for *Big Government*, while enslaving these very immigrants to cheap labor for big businesses aligned with the *political elite*.

- While only two percent of the population are gays and lesbians, their causes are being used by *Big Government* to impose its secular morality on all of society, despite over seventy percent of the population claiming to be Christian. The *ruling class* despises family, marriage, and religion since they are the greatest barriers to their vision of "human progress". Consequently, the *ruling class* will pursue any means to diminish these influences in society. For example, *The Boy Scouts of America* has been pressured to allow gay adult leaders. Just as occurred in the *Catholic Church*, this could lead to the *Boy Scouts'* demise once some of these gay leaders are exposed as having become pedophiles.

- *Global warming* or *climate change*, despite contradictory scientific evidence, is advocated by *Big Government* and their advocates because "only government can solve this problem". This gives government even more power through regulations and spending on *green energy*-focused big businesses.

Big Government's power is wielded through its more than 450 federal administrative agencies that affect every facet of our lives. These agencies employ over 2.7 million government workers and have created 175,496 pages of regulations that are spread out over 235 volumes as of 2013.[14] The administrative agencies are free to exercise legislative power, can interpret any ambiguous statutory provisions which are then even binding on the Supreme Court, and have the executive power to enforce its laws as they alone have interpreted them.[15] They can issue *Administrative Subpoenas* for papers, e-mails, and other private property, which are warrants issued without probable cause and without review before neutral judges.[16] In essence, *We the People* are ruled by a one-branch, sovereign *Administrative State* run by unelected "experts" who are not accountable to anyone. Chief Justice John Roberts stated: *"The Framers could hardly have envisioned...the authority administrative agencies now hold over our economic, social, and political activities."*[17] The only recourse we have to reign in this unconstitutional, unaccountable bureaucracy is for us, *We the People,* to do it ourselves.

---

[5] Friedrich A. Hayek, Bruce Caldwell, ed., *The Road to Serfdom: Text and Documents--The Definitive Edition, The Collected Works of F. A. Hayek,* Volume 2 (Chicago: University of Chicago Press, 2007), Title.

[6] Barbara Boland, *$174K-Per-Year Congressmen Will Get Special Obamacare Subsidy*, CNSNews, http://www.cnsnews.com/news/article/barbara-boland/174k-year-congressmen-will-get-special-obamacare-subsidy (November 15, 2013).

[7] Fox News, *Tourists to be shut out from national parks, monuments under government shutdown*, Fox News, http://www.foxnews.com/politics/2013/10/01/tourists-would-be-shut-out-from-national-parks-monuments-if-government-shuts/ (October 1, 2013).

[8] David Kocieniewski, "G.E.'s Strategies Let It Avoid Taxes Altogether," *New York Times*, March 24, 2011.

[9] Juliet Eilperin, Zachary A. Goldfarb, "IRS officials in Washington were involved in targeting of conservative groups", *The Washington Post*, May 13, 2013 (https://www.washingtonpost.com/politics/obama-denounces-reported-irs-targeting-of-conservative-groups/2013/05/13/a0185644-bbdf-11e2-97d4-a479289a31f9_story.html).

[10] Angelo M. Codevilla, *AMERICA'S RULING CLASS — AND THE PERILS OF REVOLUTION*, The American Spectator, http://spectator.org/articles/39326/americas-ruling-class-and-perils-revolution (July-August, 2010 Issue).

[11] Louis Jacobson, *Are there more welfare recipients in the U.S. than full-time workers?*, PunditFact, http://www.politifact.com/punditfact/statements/2015/jan/28/terry-jeffrey/are-there-more-welfare-recipients-us-full-time-wor/ (January 28, 2015).

[12] Patrick Howley, *Obama Group To Train 10,000 Community Organizers In Search For Next 'Organizer-In-Chief'*, The Daily Caller, http://dailycaller.com/2014/12/28/obama-group-to-train-10000-community-organizers-in-search-for-next-organizer-in-chief/ (December 28, 2014).

[13] Dustin Howard, *Will the Senate stop DOJ's community organizing bonanza?*, NetRightDaily, http://netrightdaily.com/2015/11/will-the-senate-stop-dojs-community-organizing-bonanza/ (November 13, 2015).

---

[14] Charles J. Cooper, *Confronting the Administrative State*, National Affairs, http://www.nationalaffairs.com/publications/detail/confronting-the-administrative-state (Fall, 2015).

[15] http://www.nationalaffairs.com/publications/detail/confronting-the-administrative-state.

[16] Mark J. Fitzgibbons, *How America Failed to Keep the Republic*, American Thinker, http://www.americanthinker.com/articles/2015/11/how_america_failed_to_keep_the_republic.html (November 12, 2015).

[17] http://www.nationalaffairs.com/publications/detail/confronting-the-administrative-state.

Chapter 2

==================

Our Story – American Exceptionalism

"We hold these truths to be self-evident, that all men are created equal, that they are endowed by their Creator with certain unalienable rights, that among these are life, liberty and the pursuit of happiness. ... That to secure these rights, governments are instituted among men, deriving their just powers from the consent of the governed." – **Declaration of Independence**

"The American dream is not that every man must be level with every other man. The American dream is that every man must be free to become whatever God intends he should become." – **Ronald Reagan**

Most of us are either immigrants or descendants of immigrants who came to this country to experience *American Exceptionalism*, i.e., to have freedoms and pursue equal opportunities to the best of their abilities, unencumbered by government. Immigrants recognized that hard work and prudent risks in the United States would result in a better standard of life for them, their children, and their grandchildren. These people realized that only in the United States was it possible for individuals to appropriately benefit from their studies, hard work, and a willingness to take risks. They valued the many individual freedoms afforded citizens of the United States, including freedom to achieve, *freedom of speech*, and *freedom of religion*. Eager for these freedoms, a diverse group of immigrants from all over the world learned English and melded into a society at large that became known as the *Melting Pot*, i.e., *"E pluribus unum"*, a phrase that appears on the *Great Seal of the United States* and means *"Out of many, one."*

Once in the United States, these immigrants or descendants thereof pursued economic opportunities and started families. Those willing to take risks and work hard started businesses. They rarely viewed themselves as victims when they encountered obstacles or setbacks. Instead, they learned from their experiences and became stronger. They recognized that risk and failure are necessary steps to achieving success. Each generation was better off than the previous one. Everyone's standard of life improved, even though inequalities existed due to differences in talents, ambitions, and work ethics.

Many gave back generously to their communities with charitable donations and by volunteering their time, dispelling the notion that *American Exceptionalism* promotes greed. These days, households headed by *limited government* advocates give 30% more to charity than households headed by those who believe in *Big Government*[18]. Also, people living in the top five *limited government* oriented states are 51% more likely to volunteer than those in the top five *Big Government* oriented states.[19] Furthermore, business-owning entrepreneurs give over 80% more to charity than the rest of the population. [20] In the United States, entrepreneurship and philanthropy have always been closely linked, as evidenced by Andrew Carnegie of the past and Bill Gates in the present.

Through *American Exceptionalism,* the United States became the wealthiest and most successful nation in the world. The "poor" in the United States have a much higher standard of living than in the past and relative to people of other nations.[21] Based on 2011 Census Bureau data, one in seven people (46.7 million) had income below the federal "poverty" level. Of these "poor" households, 42% owned their own homes, nearly three-fourths had a car or truck, 80% had air conditioning, 92% had a microwave, 96% had a TV (almost two-thirds with cable or satellite), nearly two-thirds had at least one DVD player, half had a personal computer, 41% had Internet access, over 50% had cell phones, and more than half had video gaming systems for their children.[22] In general, the standard of living is consistently higher for the poor in market-based societies than those economies with heavy government intervention and redistribution of wealth.

Many of the countries these immigrants left behind were dictatorial, communist, or socialist. They exemplify all-powerful, centralized governments comprised of *elite politicians* who are aligned with big business and special interests. These governments value conformity and dependence. They promise to take care of their citizens from "cradle to grave", but require redistribution of wealth from their more productive citizens to the less productive constituency, since government does not create wealth. This government intrusion on the free market ignores the inevitable cause-and-effect of such wealth transfers. It ignores that humans, unlike animals and inanimate objects, can rationally think about consequences of wealth transfer and act accordingly. The Austrian economist, Ludwig von Mises, stated that human action will attempt to substitute *"a more satisfactory situation for a less satisfactory one."*[23] In 1990, for example, when the U.S. Census Bureau asked the poor who were receiving unemployment payments why they were not working, only four percent gave *"an inability to find work"* as a reason.[24] With redistribution of wealth, society at large will experience a trend from more productive citizens to less productive citizens and an associated decline in overall standard of living, as was the case with the countries of the aforementioned immigrants.

I can personally attest to these realities. In 1961, my parents and their three sons came to the United States from Germany in pursuit of *American Exceptionalism*. They recognized that only in the United States could their sons have unlimited opportunities to realize their full potential. My parents did this at great personal risk, since they did not speak English, were unfamiliar with the culture, and had no guarantee of economic success. At times, my father worked two or three jobs as a cabinetmaker in order to support our family, buy a house, and pay college expenses. Our career choices would have been greatly limited in socialist Germany, where only the wealthy elite could attend college, and government rules and regulations would have prevented us from pursuing many career options.

My brothers and I owe much to our parents and to *American Exceptionalism*. With an equal opportunity for all, we were able to pursue our dreams through hard work and by taking risks. One of us started a small business, one pursued a career in corporate America, and one worked for a small local business. Each of us started families with the hope that our children would also be able to experience *American Exceptionalism*.

----

[18] Nicholas D. Kristof, "Bleeding Heart Tightwads," *New York Times*, December 20, 2008.

[19] Tony Listi, *Who is More Compassionate: Conservatives or Liberals?*, Conservative Colloquium, https://conservativecolloquium.wordpress.com/2008/05/15/who-is-more-compassionate-conservatives-or-liberals/ (May 15, 2008).

[20] Guinevere Nell, Paul Winfree and James Sherk, *Free-Market Philanthropy: The Social Aspect of Entrepreneurship*, The Heritage Foundation, http://www.heritage.org/research/reports/2008/09/freemarket-philanthropy-the-social-aspect-of-entrepreneurship (September 16, 2008).

[21] Tim Worstall, *Astonishing Numbers: America's Poor Still Live Better Than Most Of The Rest Of Humanity*, Forbes, http://www.forbes.com/sites/timworstall/2013/06/01/astonishing-numbers-americas-poor-still-live-better-than-most-of-the-rest-of-humanity/ (June 1, 2013).

22 Robert Rector and Rachel Sheffield, *Understanding Poverty in the United States: Surprising Facts About America's Poor*, The Heritage Foundation, http://www.heritage.org/research/reports/2011/09/understanding-poverty-in-the-united-states-surprising-facts-about-americas-poor (September 13, 2011).

23 Thomas E. Woods Jr., *The Church and the Market: A Catholic Defense of the Free Economy* (Lenham, Maryland: Lexington Books, 2005), 16.

24 Thomas E. Woods Jr., *Race, Inequality, and the Market - The Free Market Is Not the Source of Black Underachievement*, Foundation for Economic Education, http://fee.org/freeman/race-inequality-and-the-market/ (October 1, 2002).

Chapter 3

==================

Meet Thy Neighbor

"You and I have a rendezvous with destiny. We will preserve for our children this, the last best hope of man on earth, or we will sentence them to take the first step into a thousand years of darkness. If we fail, at least let our children and our children's children say of us we justified our brief moment here. We did all that could be done."
– **Ronald Reagan**

"Never doubt that a small group of thoughtful committed citizens can change the world; indeed, it's the only thing that ever has."
- **Margaret Mead, an American cultural anthropologist**

"Nobody Makes a Bigger Mistake Than He Who Did Nothing Because He Could Only Do a Little." - **Edmund Burke**

How to get started as an activist for *limited government*, the rule of law, and the U.S. Constitution? It is actually quite simple based on searching-and-reapplying the learnings from

Harvard Professor Marshall Ganz's course on *Community Organizing* and Midwest Academy's book, *Organizing for Social Change*. Start by gathering in your house a group of 10-15 family members, friends, neighbors, and acquaintances who share your values and principles, even though they may differ on issues. You can also use the *Voter Registration Records,* discussed in Chapter 14, to identify like-minded neighbors in your neighborhood. The purpose of the gathering is to create awareness of our current predicament, focus on the threats to our values and principles, and start the discussion of what actions can be pursued at the local, state, or federal level to deal with these threats. In subsequent chapters, this book lists many potential actions that can be discussed and considered. Based on dynamics in the 2015 presidential campaigns, it is obvious that many people are frustrated with the political status quo but do not know what to do. By inviting people to your *Neighborhood Meetings,* you will counter their feelings of isolation with an experience of solidarity in addition to providing an outlet for their frustrations.

As is typical in any relationship, when you hold *Neighborhood Meetings,* it is important to focus on engaging both the hearts and minds of attendees to instruct and inspire. All too often, those favoring *limited government*, the rule of law, and the U.S. Constitution focus too much on just engaging the mind. Hearts are engaged by sharing our stories and hopes with each other and realizing that we share a common bond with each other based on these foundational shared values and principles. At the *Neighborhood Meeting,* start by sharing what values and principles have guided your life thus far and the hopes you have for your children and grandchildren. You will quickly notice commonalities among attendees, regardless of race, religion, gender, etc. Only then will you have created a relationship for action to which attendees are willing to commit, based on shared futures and consequences of a shared past. History has shown us that citizens enlist in fights because of their ideals, but prevail because of loyalty to the people beside them and a commitment to those they love. It is these loved ones who have to live with the consequences of their actions or non-actions. Strong relational communities are capable of collaborative actions of all kinds. Robert Heinlein, the famous science fiction writer and author of *Take Back Your Government*, stated that in politics, the emotional factor increases any other assets by a factor of ten, trumping Napoleon's stated three to one factor in war.

As you conduct *Neighborhood Meetings*, rest assured that people are *"hungering for something"* to fix the mess we have in this country, not just platitudes and promises from politicians. This is evidenced by the many polls in which close to two-thirds of the people, regardless of political party affiliation, indicate that government has grown too large and too powerful.[25] Furthermore, about eighty percent of people polled now view the *American Dream* as out of reach[26], recognizing that it takes much more effort today to get ahead than it did for prior generations. They also recognize that the political system is non-responsive to their needs. Lastly, recognize that by advocating liberty and equal opportunity, you have the moral high ground relative to those advocating *Big Government* and crony-capitalism.

Once the emotional relational bond has been formed, it is time to move on to identifying threats to your existing and envisioned life stories and to identify possible actions. In essence, the goal is to mobilize feelings that facilitate action and challenge feelings that inhibit action. One way to counter apathy is with anger precipitated by outrage and indignation at injustices relative to your values, principles, and moral order. A hope that our values and principles can be defended will give attendees courage to act. Initially, these actions may just focus on further growing the movement through more *Neighborhood Meetings*. That is fine! Eventually, though, specific actions are required to deal with the threats to our future, our children's future, and our grandchildren's future. This is accomplished through a continuation of individual freedoms achieved through *limited government*, the rule of law, and adherence to the U.S. Constitution at the local, state, and federal levels. In subsequent chapters, this book lists many potential actions that can be discussed and considered. Additionally, make sure to brainstorm with attendees any other possible actions. You may be surprised at the creativity and diversity of ideas. Diversity of attendees is an asset, rather than an obstacle.

Do not be afraid to initially limit your actions, such as simply pursuing a local political goal in order to ensure success. It will build confidence among those involved and embolden them to gradually pursue more difficult goals. Additionally, do not forget to collaborate with other concerned community groups or existing organizations, where it makes sense, to leverage each other's resources in pursuit of a goal. Considering that your resources are volunteers, make sure to match their passions and interests with appropriate actions to ensure success. Do not forget that good actions are fun, motivational, and simple. Lastly, ensure that you assign volunteers with responsibilities to successfully complete actions, instead of simply assigning tasks. It will be more satisfying for volunteers and builds leadership capabilities. Experienced members of the group can make periodic assessments of progress and provide coaching, as needed.

Of course, getting together as neighbors has many positives associated with it. Relationships can only be built face-to-face, not through electronic social media. Too many of us are isolated from our neighbors, when in fact, during these hard times, we should check on our neighbors to assure that they are okay and help them if needed. We need to tear down artificial fences and prejudices that the *elite politicians* and media have created to divide us. In fact, neighborliness is a key part of *American Exceptionalism*. I personally experienced this when I came to the United States as an immigrant child in 1961.

Importantly, ask attendees to hold similar meetings to reach even more people and choose the more extroverted attendees to act as facilitators in those subsequent meetings. Just imagine the cumulative power that will be achieved if regular folks throughout our nation initiate these *Neighborhood Meetings*! Importantly, this values and principle-based approach requires no central leadership but will make a difference from the cumulative effect of all the local, state, and federal actions. *Neighborhood Meetings* can quickly become a national force to be reckoned with during the presidential election year of 2016 and beyond. We are the majority and we can win if everyone pulls in the same direction. Success will be based on the sum total of all our individual efforts, one neighborhood at a time. I am reminded of the movie, *Meet John Doe*, in which local citizen clubs grew virally into a national movement.

Let us make it happen! We have an obligation to preserve the *American Dream* for our children and pass on a more vibrant country to them. So I ask you, who of you will start to conduct *Neighborhood Meetings* in your neighborhood? Who will lead and advocate making it a movement in your community, county, state, and nationally? Which *limited government* organization with national reach will help facilitate this goal?

Neighborhood Meeting Successes

Clearly, we must learn from those advocating *Big Government*, such as *Organizing for America*, based on their successes to date, and from *Community Organizing* practices in general. I recognized this from my opposition research in mid-2012 during which I discovered the importance of *Neighborhood Meetings*. Those who advocate for *Big Government* call them *House Meetings*.

Some of you may have heard of *House Meetings* as part of *Organizing for America*, but probably had no idea that this has been a secret weapon of *Big Government* advocates' campaigns to win elections and influence policy. In fact, I recall a presentation I gave to a Florida *limited government* leaders' conference in Orlando during which some leaders joked about attending these *OFA House Parties*. At the time, they did not realize how integral these parties were to success.

In contrast to most *limited government* meetings which tend to focus on education and information sharing, *House Meetings* engage the hearts and minds of attendees, foster strong commitments to action, and are used to grow the network. They accomplish this by inviting people who are interested in learning more about a topic, having everyone share their personal life story, highlighting commonalities of these stories, identifying threats to the groups' common story, brainstorming actions the group can pursue, and obtaining personal commitments to actions. Importantly, attendees are made to feel as victims of outside interests by the trained *Community Organizing* facilitators. The meeting facilitator, by observing attendees, also identifies new local leaders to perpetuate the *House Meeting* methodology throughout the community.

Harvard's Professor Marshall Ganz is the mastermind behind this organizing technique, elements of which are summarized in his fall 2009 *Ganz Organizing* class notes. Ganz has been a key advisor to presidential campaigns since prior to the 2008 election. He is not only responsible for the *transformational* messaging in the campaigns, but with *House Meetings* in 2012, created the largest ground game ever amassed for an election. Professor Ganz is also behind the *New Organizing Institute* (*Wellstone Action* as of October, 2015) website focused on training *Community Organizers*. It is an excellent website with many insightful training videos. I suggest you check it out!

An anecdotal example from one of the videos on the *New Organizing Institute* website helps you understand how this methodology works. It caught my attention since it involves a large corporation for which I worked for close to thirty years. A trained *Community Organizing* facilitator targeted a small town in northeast Pennsylvania. He went into the community and met with pastors to learn about community issues. He then had these pastors set up an initial *House Meeting*. Using the *House Meeting* methodology, they quickly identified the large corporation as someone who takes advantage of the local Hispanic population. Brainstorming identified that an attending priest owned stock in this corporation and that he would take some of the local Hispanics to the next shareholder's meeting. The priest was called upon at this shareholders meeting and he allowed one of the Hispanic attendees to address the CEO in Spanish. She complained that, although she cannot even speak English, her hard work for the corporation helps to put food on both the CEO's and her own family tables. As a result of this meeting, the corporation donated millions of dollars to the community through the *Community Organizing* groups to teach English to the Hispanic community. However, you can be assured that much of the money intended for teaching English went into expanding *Community Organizing* in this town.

Organizing for America has now been transformed into *Organizing for Action*, a nonprofit 501(c)(4) advocacy group to advance President Obama's agenda after office in 2017. The First Lady made this announcement in a video message to supporters, calling the move *"the next phase in our movement for change"*[27]. *Organizing for Action* plans to train an additional 10,000 *Community Organizers* in 2015[28].

Yet another example of the effectiveness of *House Meetings* is described in Harvard Professor Ganz's course notes. It pertains to the *1987 Pelosi for Congress* campaign in San Francisco. Six organizers held eighty-seven *House Meetings* which were attended by six hundred people in just three weeks. From these, they were able to recruit one hundred ten leaders needed for the *Get-Out-The-Vote* effort for the entire congressional district. [29]

---

[25] Joy Wilke, *Americans' Belief That Gov't Is Too Powerful at Record Level*, Gallup, http://www.gallup.com/poll/164591/americans-belief-gov-powerful-record-level.aspx (September 23, 2013).

[26] David Lightman, *American dream seen as out of reach*, McClatchy-Marist Poll, http://www.mcclatchydc.com/news/nation-world/national/economy/article24763519.html (February 13, 2014).

[27] Michelle Obama, *The First Lady on the Launch of Organizing for Action*, https://www.youtube.com/watch?feature=player_embedded&v=HYT68 Uii1dk#t=0s (January 18, 2013).

[28] Patrick Howley, *Obama Group To Train 10,000 Community Organizers In Search For Next 'Organizer-In-Chief'*, The Daily Caller, http://dailycaller.com/2014/12/28/obama-group-to-train-10000-community-organizers-in-search-for-next-organizer-in-chief/ (December 28, 2014).

[29] https://annastarrrose.files.wordpress.com/2011/06/ganz-course-notes.pdf, 41.

Chapter 4

==================

Strategy – What to do now?

"... Those who profess to favor freedom, and yet deprecate agitation, are men who want crops without plowing up the ground...Power concedes nothing without a demand. It never did and it never will...The limits of tyrants are prescribed by the endurance of those whom they oppress."

- Frederic Douglas, letter to an abolitionist associate, 1849

"If you will not fight for the right when you can easily win without bloodshed; if you will not fight when your victory will be sure and not too costly; you may come to the moment when you will have to fight with all the odds against you and only a precarious chance of survival. There may even be a worse case. You may have to fight when there is no hope of victory, because it is better to perish than to live as slaves."

- Winston Churchill's challenge to England's citizens

Since our objective is to defend and preserve *American Exceptionalism* and America's founding principles against an attempt to fundamentally transform the United States towards a nonexistent utopian vision, our grand strategy must be to engage the opposition on all fronts, i.e., socially, culturally, economically, and politically. In essence, we are attempting to limit government's power over our lives, preserve our individual liberty, and foster prosperity for younger people and future generations. In contrast, the *elites'* primary objective is to consolidate power over us and exploit us through the power and enormous resources of government. Consequently, our strategy or efforts can no longer be limited to a mere focus on winning elections and issues, but must include ongoing actions by each of us to deal with the *elite's* biased media, educational institutions, and *Social Justice* religions. While these *elite* institutions may control the current national narrative, they do not represent most Americans' values and principles.

Since 2009, *TheVoicesOfAmerica.org* has primarily focused on proven, effective *Neighborhood Organizing* mechanics for winning elections. In this book, we are now also focusing on non-election related strategies and tactics. We have done much research and read numerous books to prepare each detailed strategic action and tactic in the subsequent chapters. These actions will teach you how to challenge the prevailing *Big Government* initiatives and propaganda espoused by *elites*. Our research includes reverse engineering methodologies that have allowed *Big Government elites* to succeed with only about twenty percent of the population in support of their agenda. It is important to recognize that we, the *Silent Majority*, have many more people and can reverse the *Big Government elite's* advance with our sheer numbers. While we do not have much money, history and *Big Government* activists have shown us that much can be achieved by involved people instead of having to rely on money, but it requires that all of us engage in this battle. We will be aided by the fact that our values and principles are founded in fairness and in truth.

As part of your *Neighborhood Meeting,* attempt to discern which strategies and tactics from those listed in this book are of greatest interest to attendees. You will obtain passionate commitment from attendees only if they agree that the strategies and tactics are of interest, easy to understand, non-divisive among attendees, consistent with attendees' values and vision, worthwhile, and likely to make a difference. If at all possible, make sure that the targets of your strategies and tactics are individuals or decision makers, since not much is accomplished targeting institutions or companies at large. Our opposition considers this insight fundamental to organizing and calls it *"Personalize the target"*. It works because individuals have feelings, such as a sense of ambition, fairness, guilt, fear, vanity, or loyalty. Institutions or companies do not. A secondary target can be someone who has more power over the primary target than you do, such as a purchasing agent of products from the targeted corporation or a public official who can end contracts.

Also be aware of yet another insight from Saul Alinsky's *Rules for Radicals*, that the real action in strategy can be the reaction by the opposition or other actors to your strategies and tactics. Saul Alinsky further stated that through activism, the enemy should be made to *"live up to their (sic) own book of rules"*[30] and advocated to use the system's inability to do so as a means to discredit capitalism and replace it with socialism. We have certainly seen both of these opposition strategies successfully applied over the last decades, resulting in our current predicament. Now we need to use these same strategic insights for our own purposes.

It is important to note that all governmental power and "wealth" through taxation requires assistance from constituents. Even totalitarian dictators rely on support from the ruled constituency. The government's power can thus be controlled to the extent constituents impose limits on the government's power, withhold their consent to any governmental abuse of power, and organizations and institutions maintain their independence from government powers. The famous Italian historian, politician, diplomat, philosopher, humanist, and writer, Niccolo Machiavelli, stated, *"... who has the public as a whole for his enemy can never make himself secure; and the greater his cruelty, the weaker does his regime become"*[31]. Consequently, defiant constituents cannot be forced into subjection and obedience to an all-powerful government.

An easy way for your *Neighborhood Meeting* group to discern which strategies and tactics to pursue is to: 1) brainstorm all potential strategies and tactics, 2) discuss each strategy and tactic led by those advocating the strategy and tactic, 3) have each attendee rate each of the strategies and tactics using a 1 (low) to 10 (high) rating for value of benefit and effort, and lastly, 4) sort the combined group's Value/Effort ratio scores for each of the strategies and tactics to identify high value, low effort actions to pursue. Before deciding to focus on a given strategy and tactic, it is prudent to assess one's strengths and weaknesses relative to the strategy and tactic since this will allow discovery of possible threats as well as identify opportunities, such as forming alliances.

Once you decide on a strategy focus area for the group, move on to defining specific tactics. These should identify who does what, to whom, and why the target will make concessions to stop the tactic. Tactics should be fun and be within the experience and comfort level of your group, but outside the comfort area of your intended target. Specific tactics can consist of meetings with the target individual, public meetings/hearings, media events, negotiations, or elections. Once specific tactics are identified, be sure to ask people directly for commitment to pursue the agreed upon tactics. As you implement your strategies and tactics, you will grow your group as other constituents align with your cause. You may also form alliances with groups that have similar interests.

Be aware though, as you implement your strategies and tactics, of tactical tricks your targets may use to defer or undermine your demands. They may suggest that they are the wrong person, lack funding, try to turn you against your allies, or attempt to negotiate a lesser outcome. Similarly, they may want you to join them or even appoint you to a committee for further investigation. Avoid all these trappings and persist in having your demands satisfied!

---

[30] Richard Poe, *The Cloward-Piven Strategy*, DiscoverTheNetworks.org, http://www.discoverthenetworks.org/Articles/theclowardpivenstrategyp oe.html (2005).

---

[31] Father Leslie J. Walker, ed., *The Discourses of Niccolo Machiavelli* (London: Routledge, 2013), 54.

Chapter 5

=================

Media - Tell the Truth

"If a nation expects to be ignorant and free, in a state of civilization, it expects what never was and never will be."
- Thomas Jefferson to Charles Yancey, 1816

"A nation of well-informed men who have been taught to know and prize the rights which God has given them cannot be enslaved. It is in the region of ignorance that tyranny begins." **- Ben Franklin**

"Truth will ultimately prevail where there is (sic) pains to bring it to light." **- George Washington**

American democracy cannot survive without an objective and unbiased press. Unfortunately, the *elite* mainstream and social media, where most Americans get their news, exhibit an unprecedented *Big Government Establishment* agenda bias, i.e., one that represents the *political elite* and their affiliated big businesses and institutions. Each of us interested in continuing the *American Exceptionalism*, as established by our nation's *Founding Fathers*, must engage these biased news sources and hold them accountable to the truth. This is something any one of us or any *Neighborhood Meeting* group can engage in. People within groups can even decide to focus on certain topics as subject-matter experts, based on their interests and knowledge.

The existence of a free and objective press has always been recognized as an important foundation of democracy. An unfettered and free press is the best guarantee for a free society. This right is protected by our First Amendment, which states, *"Congress shall make no law respecting an establishment of religion, or prohibiting the free exercise thereof; or abridging the freedom of speech, or of the press; or the right of the people peaceably to assemble, and to petition the government for a redress of grievances."* In 1974, Supreme Court Justice Potter Stewart stated that the primary purpose of the First Amendment was *"to create a fourth institution outside the government as an additional check on the three official branches"*[32].

The *Founding Fathers* recognized that it is a fundamental right of citizens to be informed about all sides of an issue without government interference. A self-governing society relies on truthful information and an open exchange of views in order to make decisions. To that point, Abraham Lincoln stated, *"Let the people know the facts, and the country will be safe."* Consequently, it is imperative that journalists report fair renditions of the truth, without political bias or regard to the popular mood. Additionally, the press should be able to collect and report news without fear or favor from the government or its officials. Thomas Jefferson felt so strongly about the importance of a free press that he stated, *"If it were left to me to decide whether we should have a government without a free press or a free press without a government, I would prefer the latter."*

Much of the public narrative in society is driven by news reporting, which has unfortunately become ever more biased with an unmistakable *Big Business Establishment* agenda representing the *political elite* and their affiliated big businesses and institutions. Many news sources appear to collude in that they use similar talking points when reporting the news, as evidenced by use of identical keywords. Despite being in the majority, many times the *Silent Majority* is made to feel powerless against societal forces by these cultural *Establishment elites*. The *Establishment elites* cite "fairness" as a cause, when it is you and your neighbors, the *Silent Majority*, who are not being treated fairly through unfair taxation, burdensome regulations, and intrusion into every dimension of your private lives and freedoms. Facts no longer appear to be held to the same high journalistic standard, as evidenced by much incorrect and biased reporting. In September, 2012 Brent Bozell, president of the *Media Research Center*, stated, *"In the quarter century since the Media Research Center was established to document liberal media bias, there has never been a more brazen and complete attempt by the liberal so-called 'news' media to decide the outcome of an election."* Therefore, it should be of no surprise that in September, 2015 Gallup reported that only four out of ten Americans trusted mass media.[33] This poll ties 2014 and 2012 for the lowest trust levels.

The *Media Research Center*[34] identifies the following methods used by reporters to bias their reporting: 1) Bias by Commission: a pattern of passing along assumptions or errors that tend to support a certain point of view, 2) Bias by Omission: ignoring facts that tend to disprove support for a certain point of view, or that support the opposite, 3) Bias by Story Selection: a pattern of highlighting news stories that coincide with the agenda supporting a certain point of view while ignoring stories that coincide with the agenda of those opposed to the favored point of view, 4) Bias by Placement: a pattern of placing news stories so as to downplay information supportive of those who oppose the media's biased point of view, 5) Bias by the Selection of Sources: including more sources in a story who support one view over another. This bias can also be seen when a reporter uses such phrases as "experts believe", "observers say", or "most people think", 6) Bias by Spin: emphasizing aspects of a policy favorable to a certain point of view without noting aspects favorable to those who oppose the advocated point of view; putting out an interpretation consistent with the advocated point of view of what an event means while giving little or no time or space to explain an opposing interpretation, 7) Bias by Labeling: attaching a label to those who oppose the advocated point of view but not to those who support the point of view; using more extreme labeling for opponents to the advocated point of view than for those who agree; identifying a liberal person or group as an "expert" or as independent, 8) Bias by Policy Recommendation or Condemnation: when a reporter goes beyond reporting and endorses the advocated point of view of which policies should be enacted, or affirms the criticism consistent with the point of view of current or past policies.

You might ask, where do Americans get their news? Of the 55% of Americans who obtain their news from TV[35], evening network newscasts from ABC, CBS, and NBC dominate with a four-to-one advantage[36] over the highest rated shows on the three cable news channels (CNN, Fox News, and MSNBC). Online news sources have surpassed radio and newspapers[37], with respective audiences of 39%, 33%, and 29%. For American adults under thirty, social media has far surpassed newspapers and equals TV[38] as a primary source of daily news. Net, the *Big Government Establishment* bias of TV's evening network news is complimented by the fact that many more American adults get their news online or through social media, both of which are much populated by *Big Government* oriented points of view.

To counter the overwhelming *Establishment* bias in news reporting, those interested in objective reporting must engage the news media. We must correct the mainstream news' *Establishment* agenda and public narrative to ensure all citizens are privy to the truth. We must challenge the mainstream talking points with effective and accurate information. We must promote *limited government* principles, grounded in a proper understanding of economics and with logic and truth. All of this can be achieved through Letters-to-the-Editor, Op-Eds, or meetings with the editorial board. Letters-to-the-Editor is one of the most widely read sections of the newspaper, after the front page. Op-Eds allow you to share a more comprehensive point of view, although they need to be more of a general interest. Also check if the media will allow you to contribute to one of their regularly run feature stories on issues or people. Lastly, participate in the online discussions and social media. For all of these suggestions, it is helpful to get to know the media's staff, such as reporters and editors. These personal relationships and any follow-up you make will facilitate that you get the desired media coverage. You can actually help reporters do their work if your submission, based on facts and perspective, warrants it, i.e., they might run your submission as a story. Just remember that nothing is ever confidential, so watch what you share.

In addition to engaging in the news conversations to counter *Big Government Establishment* bias, citizens have further recourse by contacting news organization "ombudsmen", who are in-house critics employed to hear public complaints. A further recourse to biased reporting is to create citizens' councils that review public complaints about the press and issue verdicts. They do not carry the force of law, but tend to be covered widely, especially now with the Internet. It is also possible to pressure those who may subsidize media outlets or pressure advertisers and corporate sponsors to those media outlets with legitimate claims of biased reporting and subverting the truth. At all times, remember that the media outlets have narrow self-interests such as increasing readership/viewership and to make a profit.

Whatever you write or say, remember that your opinion is not news. Provide factual information as well as anecdotal and real people's stories to add a human interest element to your submissions. Avoid getting sued by not stating anything that is untrue or gossip and use phrases such as "allegedly" or "according to" for assertions or perspective which you would find hard to prove.

All of the above, of course, require that we access news sources other than the ones we normally view, read, or listen to. It is human nature to surround ourselves with self-reinforcing people or news. We must pursue the above-suggested corrective actions, knowing that Americans hunger for truth. For if we are not able to ensure that news media provides objective reporting as a public service, true democracy will not survive.

---

[32] Timothy E. Cook, *Governing with the News: The News Media as a Political Institution* (Chicago: University of Chicago Press, 1954), 179.

[33] Rebecca Riffkin, *Americans' Trust in Media Remains at Historical Low*, Gallup, http://www.gallup.com/poll/185927/americans-trust-media-remains-historical-low.aspx (September 28, 2015).

[34] Brent Baker, *How to Identify Liberal Media Bias*, Media Research Center, http://archive.mrc.org/books/identifybias.asp (1994).

[35] Andrew Beaujon, *Pew: Half of Americans get news digitally, topping newspapers, radio,* The Poynter Institute, http://www.poynter.org/news/mediawire/189819/pew-tv-viewing-habit-grays-as-digital-news-consumption-tops-print-radio/ (September 27, 2012).

[36] Emily Guskin and Tom Rosenstiel, *The State of the News Media 2012*, The Pew Research Center Project for Excellence in Journalism, http://www.stateofthemedia.org/2012/network-news-the-pace-of-change-accelerates/ (2012 Annual Report).

[37] http://www.poynter.org/news/mediawire/189819/pew-tv-viewing-habit-grays-as-digital-news-consumption-tops-print-radio/

[38] Jeff Sonderman, *One-third of adults under 30 get news on social networks now*, The Poynter Institute, http://www.poynter.org/news/mediawire/189776/one-third-of-adults-under-30-get-news-on-social-networks-now/ (September 27, 2012).

Chapter 6

=================

Education – A Moral Imperative!

"Upon the subject of education ... I can only say that I view it as the most important subject which we as a people may be engaged in.
 - Abraham Lincoln

"Education is the key to unlock the golden door of freedom."
- George Washington Carver

"Our freedoms will have been lost when the people are convinced that the government is a better determinant of their child's education than what they are."
- John Taylor of Caroline, member of the Virginia House of Delegates and United States Senator

Our *Big Government* run education system is failing our children and denying them the opportunity to achieve their fullest potential. Consequently, our children can no longer compete with children in other countries in an ever-expanding global economy. It is especially true for those most disadvantaged, such as African-Americans in the inner cities whose parents have the same dreams for their children as any other parent, i.e., to have their children be better off than their own generation. This is a travesty since we have a moral obligation to properly prepare our children for the future and to give them an opportunity to excel up to their maximum abilities.

The root cause for this predicament is that *elite politicians* in *Big Government* are allowing the *Teacher Unions* to have a monopoly over our education system, something considered illegal in the private sector, in return for receiving significant campaign financing. *Teacher Unions* are the most powerful entity in the Democrat Party. In essence, these *elite politicians* are sacrificing our children's education for political gains. I should note, good teachers do exist but they are beholden to the *Teacher Unions*, tend to be the exception, and generally teach in the more affluent school districts.

Consequently, it is not surprising that the public's confidence in public schools has plummeted from 58% in 1970 to 29% in 2012[39] while annual per-student expenditures, paid by taxes, have dramatically increased from $4,552 in 1970 to $11,400 in 2012.[40] This lack of confidence is corroborated by the fact that SAT testing scores are at a 40-year low.[41] The average SAT reading score is down 34 points since 1972, high school graduation rates have been stagnant since the 1970's, and American students rank in the middle of the pack among their international peers. Education performance results are even worse among minorities, with nearly half of Blacks, Hispanics, and Native Americans dropping out of high school.[42]

Despite a systemic failure to properly educate our children, this predicament is now being made worse through the nationalized *Common Core* standards. Instead of continuing to provide a liberal arts education foundation that over decades has produced unprecedented numbers of entrepreneurs relative to other countries, the *Common Core* standards' focus is on graduating capable workers and bureaucrats for big business and *Big Government*. For example, classic literature in the curriculum is increasingly being replaced with technical manuals and government regulation documents. Specifically, by the time students reach high school, seventy-five percent of reading will be "informational" texts instead of literature.[43] Attempts are now being made to change high school AP History courses away from a focus on *American Exceptionalism* to a focus on the struggle of the many diverse groups in the United States.[44] Additionally, in *Common Core,* much personal information and data is being gathered by *Big Government* bureaucrats for each student as part of the *Student Longitudinal Database System (SLDS)*[45] which tracks students from pre-school through college.

The *Common Core* standards also indoctrinate our children to the extent that they are being exposed to an agreed-upon, morally-free national construct for every aspect of life and society. They are taught that a "kind person" spreads wealth around and that we must protect the environment at all cost. Our children are being taught to expect effortless success, seek immediate gratification, expect entitlements, and resent the success of others. *Big Government* is being positioned as a hero to children, intending to right all of the world's wrongs. Consequently, *"Big Government* as the answer to all of the world's problems" will appear normal to these children as they grow up and become adults. Even traditional families are targeted as obstacles with their emphasis on parental authority, moral training, and being a source of support for children. These are not congruent with an all-powerful central government.

As evidence, I share content from the *Common Core English Literature and Writing*[46] curriculum guide for teachers. In essence, our children are being taught Harvard Professor Ganz's *Community Organizing* tactics, discussed as

Neighborhood Organizing in Chapter 3. In the first grade guide, one of the *Common Core English Literature and Writing* curriculum slides focuses on *"advocating solutions to social problems"* and *"social advocacy"* in the context of *"what makes a good neighbor"*. In another slide, the focus is on using *"emotional words"* to *"appeal to ... emotions and feelings"* so that the audience *"feels strongly about the problem so that they want to do what is being asked of them"*. In the sixth grade guide, the focus is on students learning about *"social values which unite us as a country"* with emphasis on learning about *Social Justice.* In essence, our children are being taught how to manipulate parents and others with emotions. They are being trained to become *Social Justice Community Organizers* to highlight problems and advocate for solutions that only *Big Government* can provide. In the process, parents are marginalized.

Indoctrination of children at a young age is actually quite easy.[47] Children are easily influenced since they do not know what they do not know, do not know what questions to ask, and tend to bond with and trust teachers. For example, children are taught not to pray, not to mention God in public, and to be sensitive to the practices of Muslims but not to Christians. They do not ask why the anti-Christian bias exists and why, in general, they are subjected to a "secular humanistic religion". Additionally, they do not know to ask why they are not studying the Constitution and the Federalist Papers, all foundational documents for our United States. Even our universities, who supposedly advocate diversity and *freedom of speech*, have become oppressors of both as they attempt to stop any critique of their biased *Big Government* ideas and agenda.

What to Do?

Parents

As is more extensively discussed in the book, *Waking the Sleeping Giant: How Mainstream Americans Can Beat Liberals at Their Own Game,* written by psychologists Timothy C. Daughtry and Gary R. Casselman, parents must become the first line of defense against indoctrination in schools. Instead of disputing biased and incorrect information from teachers and school books, parents need to provide correct information to their children. They must teach their children that just because a teacher or a book states something, it is not necessarily correct. Parents must focus on the text and materials and not so much on the teacher. It is important for children to learn that good people can be misinformed. Parents have an excellent opportunity to teach children how to reference multiple sources to discern truths. This will teach children critical thinking skills and an appreciation for diversity of ideas.

Parents need to also invest time and effort to teach their children that America is a good country and to teach them about American heroes and history. They can front-load liberty-loving values through strong association with and participation in Fourth of July and Memorial Day activities. Parents need to teach their children how liberty and personal responsibility are linked and how tyranny can evolve without liberty. Excellent, free online educational videos on the Constitution are available from Hillsdale College[48].

School Board

The *Silent Majority* must get involved locally with the school board to hold it accountable for educational results of the children. Clearly, it would not be prudent for parents to confront either teachers or the school board for fear of retribution against their child. But through a *Neighborhood Meeting* group, those who no longer have children in school could intervene at the school board level with knowledge gained from those neighbors who do have children in school. Groups could also pursue student surveys or focus groups to identify issues, but do so with care. Since school board members are elected officials, they will respond to appropriate public pressure. Be aware, however, that many school board members, even though they are fully responsible, are not very much aware of and involved in day-to-day operations. They often defer all of this to the school superintendent who tends to be more aligned with the *Teacher Unions*.

Silent Majority citizens should run for school board using the *Get-Out-The-Vote* method discussed in Chapter 14. In Ohio, many *Silent Majority* candidates have been elected to school boards and have now started an alternate, state-wide *Ohio School Boards Leadership Council (OSBLC)[49]* to compete with the existing statewide *Teacher Unions* oriented *School Board Association*. Only through school board involvement can the *Silent Majority* demand and achieve fairness, balance, and diversity of ideas in textbooks and in the classroom. For increased effectiveness, *Silent Majority* parents must adopt the *"speaking truth to power"* language of *Big Government* advocates when challenging the education system. Do not oppose "reform", but instead, lead it to accomplish better educational results for our children. In fact, the *Silent Majority* should build a local political movement that elects *Silent Majority* candidates, not only to school boards, but to all local positions of power, such as libraries, museums, commissioners, and local government.

Freedom of Speech

We are now witnessing an attempt by the *elite* education establishment to usurp Judeo-Christian-based morality and its associated values and principles, and replace it with their *political elite* "secular religion" based on "science", "modernism", "relativism", and "humanism". While not advocating for a new mainstream or organized religion, what is being shared with our children is still a religion as defined by Merriam-Webster's Dictionary, i.e., *"an interest, a belief, or an activity that is very important to a person or group"*. The consequence of this development is that we now have a minority of *political elite* educators imposing their worldview on the *Silent Majority's* children in schools. The purported *political elite's* advancement of diversity and tolerance does not include those who share Judeo-Christian beliefs. As we are already witnessing, this will result in the destruction of Judeo-Christian foundational elements such as family, marriage, and the "values" our children should be learning and which have served this country well since its founding.

We should note, though, that the real world occurrences described above are based on a lack of understanding by teachers and administrators of students' *First Amendment Rights*, which include *freedom of religion*. The U.S. Department of Education's own document, entitled, *"Guidance on Constitutionally Protected Prayer in Public Elementary and Secondary Schools"* (February 7, 2003)[50], clearly states that students can pray, read the Bible and other religious books, talk about their faith, organize prayer groups and religious clubs and announce their meetings, and express their faith in their classwork and homework, including expressing their faith at school events such as their graduation ceremony. Up-to-date information can also be obtained from *Catholics for Freedom of Religion* (www.cffor.org), who in collaboration with the Diocese of Rockville Centre in New York State has published an excellent pamphlet called *Free to Speak*.[51] They have provided a great service to all peoples of faith.

If faith-related school issues occur, parents can, without expense or commitment, contact the following free legal resources, who will contact the school district as warranted:

- Thomas More Society
  (https://www.thomasmoresociety.org/legal-help)
- Liberty Institute *(https://libertyinstitute.org/take-action/request-legal)*

- Alliance Defending
  (https://www.alliancedefendingfreedom.org/legal-help)

School Choice

The "simple" solution to all of the issues cited above would be to allow a market-based approach to education in which schools compete for children. However, this approach has been shut down by *elite politicians* through pressure from the *Teacher Unions,* despite many *school choice* successes. Indeed, many successful charter schools in predominantly black neighborhoods in Washington, D.C. and in New York City have been defunded and shut down.

An excellent, single-variable example of the difference between public education and charter school education was featured in an October 6, 2015 *Wall Street Journal* editorial titled, *"A Tale of Two Schools, One Building"*[52]. It contrasted the public *Wadleigh Secondary School* to the *Success Academy Harlem West* charter school, both in the same building on the west side of Harlem. At both schools, ninety-five percent of students are Black or Hispanic and have a poverty rate in excess of sixty percent. Students in both schools use the same cafeteria, gym, and playground. The only difference is that students in *Success Academy Harlem West* were lucky enough to win the admission lottery for the limited slots allocated by New York City for charter schools. Nevertheless, zero percent of students in grades six through eight at *Wadleigh Secondary School* meet state standards in math, while ninety-six percent of students at *Success Academy Harlem West* are proficient in math with eighty percent scoring at the advanced level. For perspective, New York City spends an average of $20,331 per pupil, which ranks number two in per-pupil spending among the one hundred largest school districts in the country according to 2012-13 census data.

In yet another opinion article in the same *Wall Street Journal*, titled *"Zuckerberg's $100 Million Lesson*[53]*"*, it shows that infusing school districts with money with the hope of improving education is futile. Philanthropists who have given hundreds-of-millions of dollars over the years have seen no improvement. Instead of helping the students, their money was used on consultants, salaries, and pensions for teachers and administrators. More recently though, philanthropists have learned that successes can be achieved by donating monies to non-public, nonprofit schools such as charter schools discussed in the previous paragraph.

It should thus be clear that the *Silent Majority* must advocate and support *school choice*, such as parochial schools, charter schools, and home schooling, as an alternative to public schools. This is especially true for inner-city minorities whose parents recognize that in order to escape poverty, their children must at least learn basic literacy, computer skills, manners, and a sense of personal responsibility. Not even this is being accomplished today with our failed education system! Minorities must relinquish their total allegiance to the *Teacher Unions* and their affiliated *elite politicians* who have been exploiting them for political gains. Minorities, in collaboration with the broader *Silent Majority*, must demand better educational results for their children.

Higher Education

　　Big Government elite politicians now control higher education content and conduct by having full control over student loans. Language in the 2010-passed *Obamacare* makes the federal *Department of Education* the sole provider of student loans[54]. Due to high tuitions, colleges and universities must accept students with government loans to survive, thus having to submit themselves to all of the federal government's rules and regulations. Consequently, colleges and universities advocate the *Big Government political elite's* "secular religion" based on "science", "modernism", "relativism", and "humanism". In 2011, over sixty-two percent of undergraduate faculty members in colleges and universities identified themselves as either "liberal" or "far-left".[55] In 2015, "liberal" commencement speakers outnumbered "conservatives" by a factor of six to one.[56] Colleges and universities are now the least tolerant institutions for inquiry and debate, relying on student intimidation and discomfort to advocate their *Big Government elite politician* orthodoxy.[57]

Clearly, the *Big Government elite politicians'* monopolistic control over our higher education must be stopped! This can be achieved by getting the federal government out of the student loan business. We must ensure that free inquiry and speech in higher education is restored. This is what it used to mean to obtain a "liberal education". Colleges and universities should reflect the *Silent Majority* values - pluralism, diversity, opportunity, critical intelligence, openness, and fairness - which have been and still are the cornerstones of American society for most of us.

----

[39] Lindsey Burke, *Lack of Confidence in Public Schools at an All-Time High*, TheDailySignal, http://dailysignal.com//2012/06/21/lack-of-confidence-in-public-schools-at-an-all-time-high/ (June 21, 2012).

---

[40] Lindsey Burke, *Back to School: Some Surprising Education Numbers*, TheDailySignal, http://dailysignal.com//2012/08/27/back-to-school-some-surprising-education-numbers/ (August 27, 2012).

[41] Lindsey Burke, *SAT Scores at Historical Low; Education Spending at Historical High*, TheDailySignal, http://dailysignal.com//2012/09/25/sat-scores-at-historical-low-education-spending-at-historical-high/ (September 25, 2012).

[42] John M. Bridgeland, John J. DiIulio, Jr.,Karen Burke Morison, *The Silent Epidemic - Perspectives of High School Dropouts*, A report by Civic Enterprises in association with Peter D. Hart Research Associates for the Bill & Melinda Gates Foundation, https://docs.gatesfoundation.org/Documents/TheSilentEpidemic3-06Final.pdf (March, 2006).

[43] Kelly Kohls, *Common Core is bad for students and teachers: Kelly Kohls*, school board member, activist, The Plain Dealer, http://www.cleveland.com/metro/index.ssf/2013/11/no_common_core_is_bad_for_stud.html (November 10, 2013).

[44] Adam Lerner, *History class becomes a debate on America*, Politico, http://www.politico.com/story/2015/02/ap-us-history-controversy-becomes-a-debate-on-america-115381 (February 12, 2015).

[45] Jane Robbins, *Common Core & Data Collection, Truth in American Education* (TAE), http://truthinamericaneducation.com/privacy-issues-state-longitudinal-data-systems/common-core-data-collection/ (April 7, 2014).

---

[46] Neil Stevens, *Common Core: Bad Math meets Radical Politics - It's like Global Warmism, but inflicted on kids*, RedState, http://www.redstate.com/2014/04/02/common-core-bad-math-meets-radical-politics/ (April 2, 2014).

[47] Timothy Daughtry, Gary Casselman, *Waking the Sleeping Giant: How Mainstream Americans Can Beat Liberals at Their Own Game* (New York: Beaufort Books, 2012), Whole Book.

[48] Larry P. Arnn, et al., *Constitution 101: The Meaning & History of the Constitution*, Hillsdale college, http://online.hillsdale.edu/course/con101/schedule (November 6, 2015).

[49] Ohio School Board Leadership Council, *PROTECT THE FUTURE OF EDUCATION*, A voluntary, nonpartisan organization of Ohio School Board Members, Ohio School Board Candidates and Ohio citizens interested in improving education through School Boards, http://www.osblc.org/ (November 6, 2015).

[50] U.S. Department of Education, *Guidance on Constitutionally Protected Prayer in Public Elementary and Secondary Schools,* Office of Elementary and Secondary Education, http://www2.ed.gov/policy/gen/guid/religionandschools/prayer_guidance.html (February 7, 2003).

[51] Catholics for Freedom of Religion, *Free to Speak - Student Rights to Religious Expression in Public Schools*, Preserving Religious Liberty for All, http://www.drvc-faith.org/wp-content/uploads/ReligiousLibertyMaterials1.pdf (November 6, 2015).

---

[52] Nicholas Simmons, "A Tale of Two Schools, One Building", *Wall Street Journal*, October 6, 2015.

[53] James Piereson, Naomi Schaeffer Riley, "Zuckerberg's $100 Million Lesson", *Wall Street Journal*, October 5, 2015.

[54] Obamacarefacts.com, *Summary of the Health Care and Education Reconciliation Act of 2010*, Obamacare Facts, http://obamacarefacts.com/summary-of-the-health-care-and-education-reconciliation-act-of-2010/ (November 6, 2015).

[55] Mark R. Levin, *Plunder and Deceit* (New York: Simon & Schuster, Inc., Threshold Editions, 2015), 86.

[56] Levin, 89.

[57] Levin, 88.

Chapter 7

==================

Freedom of Speech

"If the freedom of speech is taken away then dumb and silent we may be led, like sheep to the slaughter." - **George Washington**

"All tyranny needs to gain a foothold is for people of good conscience to remain silent." -**Thomas Jefferson**

"Tolerance and apathy are the last virtues of a dying society."
– **Aristotle**

"Religion does not give [Americans] their taste of freedom… It singularly facilitates their use of it." – **Alexis de Tocqueville**

Have you ever wondered where *Political Correctness* comes from? Who started, advocates, and enforces *Political Correctness*? Simply stated, it is an attempt by the *political elite* and their adherents in the *Big Government Establishment*, the educational system, and the media to suppress free speech and to mold public opinion by saturating all means of mass communication with repetition of their ideology. They encourage individuals to conform and discourage them from engaging with each other in substantive discussions of beliefs, values, principles, and issues. In his essays, *First Principles of Government*[58], David Hume highlights the importance of government's control of public opinions by stating, *"Force is always on the side of the governed, the governors have nothing but opinion to support them. It is therefore on opinion only that government is founded."*

Violators of *Political Correctness* are immediately dealt with through public shaming, name-calling (such as racist, phobic, or bigot), and negative associations. The role of professional *Big Government* oriented *Community Organizers* orchestrating much of this cannot be underestimated[59]. Their intent is to produce the illusion of public opinion shifts with mass media saturation through repetition and coordinated talking points, and to drive opposing-view onlookers into submission and conformity through fear of social isolation. All of this is facilitated by today's social media through the use of "mob outrage", and by public schools and universities with their *political elite's* intolerance of free expression. This intimidation, to frighten the citizenry from confiding in each other and engaging in reasoned debates of issues, results in a weak populace without hope and with an acquired habit of obedience.[60] Importantly, as a result of this intimidation, these citizens lack self-confidence, tend to self-censure, and lack a capability to resist an all-powerful *Big Government* run by *political elites* and their aligned businesses and institutions.

Political Correctness Exposed

The methods of *Political Correctness* were imported to the United States via *Columbia University* from a German think tank called the *Institute for Social Research* (I.S.R.), but popularly known as the Frankfurt School[61]. The stated goal of the Frankfurt School was to undermine Judeo-Christian thought throughout society, calling it "abolition of culture" *(in German, Aufhebung der Kultur)*, and to implement a replacement for Judeo-Christian thought that would increase alienation among the population, thus decreasing their empathy for others, fostering narcissism, and increasing tolerance of violence.[62] It has since been used by the Soviet Union and Mao's China as a top-down means of censorship, i.e., by demanding conformity to the central government's ideological viewpoints. An excellent resource which exposes this *politically correct* methodology is the 1956 book, *The Rape of the Mind: The Psychology of Thought Control, Menticide, and Brainwashing,* by Joost A. M. Meerloo, a Dutch psychiatrist. It was based on a study of social psychology, including interviews of Nazi officers and American prisoners of war in Korea.[63] In it, Meerloo writes, *"This book attempts to depict the strange transformation of the free human mind into an automatically responding machine – a transformation which can be brought about by some of the cultural undercurrents in our present-day society as well as by deliberate experiments in the service of a political ideology."* It is as if he is describing today's world of *Political Correctness.*

The effectiveness of *Political Correctness* is best demonstrated by a simple psychology conformity experiment conducted in 1951 by Solomon Asch at Swarthmore College.[64] In it, he had groups of eight students view two cards with lines, as pictured on the right. They were asked to indicate which line on the right card corresponded with the line length on the left card. Seven of the eight students were actors 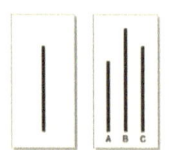 who intentionally chose the wrong answer, while the last-to-answer student was the only real subject of this study. Amazingly, 36.8% of the subject students defied their eyes and reality and chose the wrong answer espoused by the "actor" fellow students. Just think how much higher this percentage would be if the peer "actor" students could have verbally assaulted and intimidated any subject students in this test who actually dared choose the correct response?

The bottom line is that the methods and tools of *Political Correctness* are powerful! As Dr. Meerloo states in *The Rape of the Mind*, *"...he who dictates and formulates the words and phrases we use, he who is master of the press and radio, is master of the mind.*[65]*"*

Political Correctness' War on Religion

Consistent with the above, the *political elite,* through *Big Government,* have been particularly intent on diminishing the role of churches and *people of faith* in the *public square.* Notice how the *political elite,* while appealing to our sensibilities, have cleverly enabled and empowered those on the fringes of society to overwhelm mainstream values and principles and to rely on an omnipotent powerful government for enforcement. In essence, the tail is now wagging the dog, since over seventy percent of the United States population professes to be *persons of faith*[66]. Along with our use of reason and common sense, religion has been the foundation for our sense of right and wrong which is woven into the values, habits, and language of mainstream American culture. Now, the *political elite,* through the force of *Big Government,* is attempting to usurp Judeo-Christian based morality and its associated values and principles in the *public square* and replace it with its own secular "religion" based on "science", "modernism", "relativism", and "humanism". This results in the destruction of Judeo-Christian foundational elements such as family, marriage, and the values our children should be taught in schools. The purported *political elite*'s advancement of diversity and tolerance does not include those who share Judeo-Christian beliefs.

Our nation was founded on Judeo-Christian principles, as evidenced in the Declaration of Independence: *"We hold these truths to be self-evident, that all men are created equal, that they are endowed by their Creator with certain unalienable rights, that among these are life, liberty and the pursuit of happiness..."*. While acknowledging that our rights are derived from God, our *Founding Fathers* did not place Biblical morality directly into our founding documents. This ensured a separation of church and state, preventing any potential theocratic, totalitarian rule. Our *Founding Fathers* did not, however, separate God from the state. Instead, they placed God explicitly into the national life of the United States, as evidenced in inscriptions on our federal buildings and currency, in our laws, and in our mottos such as, *"In God We Trust"* and *"One Nation under God."* This conviction of our *Founding Fathers* is best exemplified by John Adams when he said, *"We have no government armed with power capable of contending with human passions unbridled by morality and religion. Avarice, ambition, revenge, or gallantry would break the strongest cords of our Constitution as a whale goes through a net. Our Constitution was made for a moral and religious people. It is wholly inadequate to the government of any other."*

History has shown us that this progression to nihilism, where good and bad are personally defined by each individual, ultimately leads to anarchy and then to a totalitarian state. Once the religious institutions' power and influence have been removed from the *public square*, only government remains as the enforcer of the state's "secular religion", since individuals alone lack such power. This was the case under socialist Nazi Germany and under Communism in Mao's China and Lenin's Russia. Even less extreme examples, such as state-sponsored socialism as practiced currently throughout Europe, show the negative effects on individual freedom, initiative, self-esteem, and standard of living, all contrary to *American Exceptionalism.*

A.D. Lindsay, in his classic 1943 book, *The Modern Democratic State,* writes that despite its frequent corruptions throughout the centuries, the Church as a distinct society provided a corrective challenge to the ambitions of the state. Specifically, *"It was perhaps equally important that the existence and prestige of the Church prevented society from being totalitarian, prevented the Omni-competent state, and preserved liberty in the only way that liberty can be preserved, by maintaining in society an organization which could stand up against the state."*

Antidote to *Political Correctness*

Stopping *Political Correctness* is as simple as just speaking up, standing your ground, and not apologizing for stating facts or your opinion. *Neighborhood Meetings*, as discussed in Chapter 3, are perhaps an easier-to-pursue initial antidote to *Political Correctness*. They facilitate discussion among family, friends, neighbors, and acquaintances of diverse beliefs, values, principles, and issues outside the control of the *political elite*. Let us ensure that we do not succumb to the *elite's* desired *"conspiracy of silence"* through their use of *Political Correctness*. As Nobel Laureate Czeslaw Milosz stated, *"In a room where people unanimously maintain a conspiracy of silence, one word of truth sounds like a pistol shot.*[67]*"* Let us start making lots of noise! In fact, let us drive public opinion by creating and advocating our own slogans that advocate the *Silent Majority's* worldview and exposes the *political elite*, such as *"help the poor, promote free markets"* or *"Social Justice = free markets"*. Just make sure our messages are aimed at the heart, not the mind.

Additionally, churches must be prodded to more actively defend the First Amendment's guaranteed *freedom of religion* in the *public square* and not just be content to have *freedom of worship* within their churches. For too long, churches have been excluded from the political process via "misunderstanding and excuses" of the 501(c)(3) nonprofit status[68]. All the while, churches have allowed assaults on religion in the *public square* by the *political elite's* government-funded third-parties such as the ACLU. These entities get paid, win or lose, by *Big Government* under the *1976 Civil Rights Act*[69]. In essence, our own tax dollars are being used by the *political elite Big Government* to fight our expression of religious beliefs in the *public square*. This is an abuse of the original intent of the *1976 Civil Rights Act*, which was designed to assist people who could not afford counsel in racially-oriented civil rights cases. This abuse must be stopped!

[58] David Hume, *Part I, Essay IV - OF THE FIRST PRINCIPLES OF GOVERNMENT*, Library of Economics and Liberty, http://www.econlib.org/library/LFBooks/Hume/hmMPL4.html (November 6, 2015).

[59] Ivan Boothe, *What online activism can learn from community organizing*, RootWork, http://rootwork.org/blog/2010/04/what-online-activism-can-learn-community-organizing (April 9, 2010).

[60] Gene Sharp, *From Dictatorship to Democracy: A Conceptual Framework for Liberation* (New York: The New Press, 2012), 5.

[61] Michael Minnicino, *The Frankfurt School and 'Political Correctness'*, Schiller Institute, http://www.schillerinstitute.org/fid_91-96/921_frankfurt.html (Winter, 1992).

[62] http://www.schillerinstitute.org/fid_91-96/921_frankfurt.html.

[63] Stella Morabito, *How To Escape The Age Of Mass Delusion*, The Federalist, http://thefederalist.com/2015/06/08/how-to-escape-the-age-of-mass-delusion/ (June 8, 2015).

[64] Wikipedia, *Asch conformity experiments*, The free encyclopedia, https://en.wikipedia.org/wiki/Asch_conformity_experiments (November 6, 2015).

---

[65] Joost A. M. Meerloo, *The Rape of the Mind: The Psychology of Thought Control, Menticide, and Brainwashing* (San Diego, CA: Progressive Press, 2009) 47.

[66] Gary Langer, *Poll: Most Americans Say They're Christian*, ABC News, http://abcnews.go.com/US/story?id=90356&page=1 (November 6, 2015).

[67] Wikiquote, *Czesław Miłosz*, Free online compendium of sourced quotations from notable people and creative works in every language, https://en.wikiquote.org/wiki/Czes%C5%82aw_Mi%C5%82osz (November 6, 2015).

[68] Peter H. Wolf, *Non-Profit Laws - Political Guidelines for 501(c)(3) and Churches*, TheVoicesOfAmerica.org, http://thevoicesofamerica.org/Non-Profit_Laws.html (November 6, 2015).

[69] American Civil Rights Union (ACRU), *The ACLU's Exploitation of the Civil Rights Attorney Fee Act*, Dedicated to protecting the civil rights of all Americans by publicly advancing a constitutional understanding of our essential rights and freedoms, http://www.theacru.org/the_aclus_exploitation_of_the/ (October 4, 2006).

Chapter 8

==================

Social Justice with Dignity

"You cannot help the poor by destroying the rich...You cannot lift the wage earner up by pulling the wage payer down. You cannot further the brotherhood of man by inciting class hatred. You cannot build character and courage by taking away people's initiative and independence. You cannot help people permanently by doing for them, what they could and should do for themselves." - **Abraham Lincoln**

"Good intentions will always be pleaded for every assumption of authority. It is hardly too strong to say that the Constitution was made to guard the people against the dangers of good intentions. There are men in all ages who mean to govern well, but they mean to govern. They promise to be good masters, but they mean to be masters." - **Daniel Webster**

"It is the right (of economic initiative) which is important not only for the individual but also for the common good. Experience shows us that the denial of this right, or its limitation in the name of an alleged "equality" of everyone in society, diminishes, or in practice absolutely destroys, the spirit of initiative, that is to say the creative subjectivity of the citizen." - **Pope John Paul II writings on economic initiative**

We have a moral obligation to provide a safety net for those among us who truly need help and to provide assistance in such a way as to maintain the dignity and self-esteem of the recipients. *Big Government,* in its failed attempt to fight poverty, instead creates dependencies. Its advocacy of *Social Justice* as a catch-all phrase is used today to advocate for equal outcomes instead of equal opportunities, requiring redistribution of wealth controlled by the *Big Government's political elite.* This centrally coordinated equal outcome goal is fundamentally flawed. It ignores human nature, basic economics, and even religious teachings of *subsidiarity,* which state that, *"matters ought to be handled by the smallest, lowest or least centralized competent authority".*[70] More effective means to achieve *Social Justice* exist and are supported by success examples. These should be emulated.

Big Government's War on Poverty, which was initiated in 1964, has been a massive moral failure. After spending over $15 trillion dollars, the poverty rate has only fallen from 14.7% in 1966 to 14.5% in 2013.[71] In 1951, just 3.8% of Americans received public aid, while in 2012, this number increased to 32.3%.[72] Between 2009 and 2015, Americans on food stamps increased by 45%.[73] Not only has *Big Government's War on Poverty* resulted in an immorally high national debt, but it has also institutionalized dependency. As an unintended consequence, it has destroyed families, especially those in black, inner-city communities.

Even churches have been deceived into advocating for this failed model of *Social Justice.* Most remarkably, they are even willing to collaborate with *Big Government* on *Social Justice* initiatives despite being forced by the secular *Big Government* to drop any references to faith or religion. This was affirmed to me personally in a debate I had during the 2012 presidential election year with an Archdiocesan Director of the Social Teaching Office. He stated, *"It is acceptable to vote for a candidate who advocates for abortion, if he supports Social Justice, as long as we are not voting for this candidate to support abortion"*. These mental gymnastics of providing equal weight to abortion and *Social Justice* are in clear violation of the

Catholic Church's core teachings which state that abortion is a non-negotiable and intrinsic evil.

The *political elite* have pursued this failed approach of dealing with complex human behavior based on a delusional belief that poverty is fixable through the scientific method, i.e., a belief that people are as predictable as the laws of physics. The following example, discussed in *The Church And The Market: A Catholic Defense of the Free Economy*[74], authored by Thomas Woods, Jr., demonstrates the difficulty of anticipating human behavior. Many view Sweden as the epitome of a successful socialist state that manages to take care of its citizens from "cradle to grave". In 1912, Sweden prohibited child labor and introduced old-age welfare. By 1935, this resulted in the lowest birthrate in Europe. Children could no longer help with family finances through work, but parents were nevertheless expected to bear the expenses of raising them. In reaction to this crisis, the Swedish government decided to financially encourage couples to have children by alleviating the cost burden of rearing children and, in essence, provided "cradle to grave" welfare to all. The unexpected consequence of this government action was that marriage rates in Sweden fell to a record low among modern nations, two-thirds of Swedes chose to live in single-person households, and over half of all Swedish births were outside of marriage. In essence, the need for a family unit no longer existed. In addition, Swedish median income by the end of the 1990s was $26,800, compared to $39,400 in the United States. Economists from the *Swedish Research Institute of Trade* indicated that *"Black people, who have the lowest income in the United States, now have a higher standard of living than an ordinary Swedish household."*[75] It appears that U.S. politicians are on the verge of successfully replicating this travesty in our very own U.S. inner cities through unsustainable *Social Justice* programs.

Yet another example discussed in Thomas Woods Jr.'s book is that the Catholic Church's *Social Justice* initiatives in South America have been a travesty. Instead of an improved standard of living, countries ended up with corrupt dictators. Venezuela's Hugo Chavez is the poster child for this scenario. To get elected, he appealed to the lower classes with demagoguery and populist promises of *Social Justice*. Since his policies were not grounded in economic reality, he was not able to deliver and Venezuela's standard of living declined. The very same people who elected Chavez are now rising up against his successor, only to be met with force. The Catholic Church has now abandoned their initiatives throughout South and Central America.

Only free-market economies can and have produced one of the greatest creations of wealth, resulting in increased life expectancies, caloric intake, literacy, education, etc. The poor within these economies have benefited much, as evidenced by better housing, health, sanitation, and declines in famine, disease, and infant mortality. Importantly, the market-based economies do not rely on government coercion and manipulation, but instead rely on a system of peaceful social cooperation.

Effective *Social Justice* Actions

Public Square

At minimum, we should engage in the public discourse of *Social Justice* with family, friends, neighbors, work associates, and in the media to counter the destructive *Big Government Social Justice* narrative. Your perspective will likely be well-received by most, since over ninety percent, regardless of political affiliation or ideology, agree with the following statement: *"Able-bodied adults that receive cash, food, housing, and medical assistance should be required to work or prepare for work as a condition of receiving those government benefits."*[76]

With politicians, we should insist that they work for proven *Social Justice* programs that reflect the complexities of human nature, maintain the self-esteem and dignity of recipients, and are sustainable. As President Reagan said, *"[t]here is no humanity or charity in destroying self-reliance, dignity, and self-respect... the very substance of moral fiber."*[77] For example, we should again emulate the successful welfare reforms implemented in 1996 by then-President Bill Clinton. These reforms required that recipients work to receive benefits and imposed limits on the length of the welfare support. In response to these reforms, welfare rolls over the next ten years dropped from 12.2 million to 4.5 million.[78] Sixty percent of mothers found jobs and left welfare, far surpassing the experts' expectations. In 2012, President Obama eliminated this work requirement with an Executive Action that went unchallenged by Congress.[79]

Church Programs

We must engage our churches' *Social Justice* organizations and have them focus on voluntary charity, consistent with Bible teachings, instead of their current focus to engage in politics and advocate for government-sponsored *Social Justice* initiatives focused on wealth redistribution.

Social Justice should be delivered as a voluntary charity that includes a sharing of religious and moral teachings, in contrast to the government's secular delivery of *Social Justice*.

Ironically, by attempting to outsource *Social Justice* to the secular government, churches will eventually destroy themselves. Government, instead of churches, will be seen by the citizenry as satisfying "cradle to grave" needs. The empty European churches are a testament to this eventual predicament. Furthermore, the typical European no longer feels a need to reach out to the poor and downtrodden, feeling that it is now the job of the government to take care of them.

Social Justice should be delivered in a way that maintains the recipient's self-esteem and dignity, while also providing foundational attributes which lead to long-term happiness. These attributes are faith, morals, and work-related skills. Such a ministry teaches those in need "to fish" instead of just giving them "fish". Many success examples exist which can be emulated by any religious group. *Homeboy Industries*[80] in California is an excellent example. Run by Jesuits, they focus on at-risk and gang-involved youth, providing them services and job-training.

The *Doe Fund*[81] in New York City is yet another excellent example where the homeless reclaim their lives through work, while also regaining dignity, self-esteem, morals, and principles. For over thirty years, instead of giving up on these homeless, this program has given them transitional work, starting with cleaning streets and sidewalks, supplemented with skills training and GED education courses. Instead of *"the soft bigotry of low expectations"[82]*, as articulated by President George W. Bush, the *Doe Fund* holds participants to the same standards as the well-off. Most importantly, it gives participants hope that they, too, can pursue the *American Dream*.

---

[70] Widipedia, *Subsidiarity*, The Free Encyclopedia, https://en.wikipedia.org/wiki/Subsidiarity_(Catholicism) (November 7, 2015).

[71] Arthur C. Brooks, *The Conservative Heart: How to Build a Fairer, Happier, and More Prosperous America* (New York: Broadside Press, HarperCollins Publishers, 2015), 63.

[72] Brooks, 64.

[73] Brooks, 142.

[74] Thomas E. Woods Jr., *The Church and the Market: A Catholic Defense of the Free Economy* (Lenham, Maryland: Lexington Books, 2005), 150 - 151.

75   Dale Franks, *Slackernomics: Basic Economics for People Who Think Economics is Boring* (Bloomington, IN: iUniverse, 2004), 29.

76 Brooks, 72.

77 Jim Hayes, *The Original Reagan Conservative: Ronald Reagan's Conservative Ideas In His Own Words* (Seattle: CreateSpace Independent Publishing Platform – Amazon, 2008), 121.

78 Betsy Myers, *Take the Lead: Motivate, Inspire, and Bring Out the Best in Yourself and Everyone Around You*, Reprint Edition (New York: Atria Books - Simon & Schuster, 2012), 83.

79 Robert Rector, Rachel Sheffield, *Ending Work for Welfare: An Overview*, The Heritage Foundation, http://www.heritage.org/research/reports/2012/08/obama-administration-ends-welfare-reform-as-we-know-it (August 29, 2012).

80 Homeboy Industries *provides hope, training, and support to formerly gang-involved and previously incarcerated men and women allowing them to redirect their lives and become contributing members of our community.*, http://homeboyindustries.org/ (November 7, 2015).

81 The Doe Fund, *Ready, Willing, and Able - Provide the homeless with a hand up, not a handout*, http://www.doe.org/ (November 7, 2015).

82 New York Times, *Excerpts From Bush's Speech on Improving Education*, http://www.nytimes.com/1999/09/03/us/excerpts-from-bush-s-speech-on-improving-education.html (September 3, 1999).

Chapter 9

==================

Advocacy with Heart

"The advancement and diffusion of knowledge is the only guardian of true liberty." – **James Madison**

"I know no safe depository of the ultimate powers of the society but the people themselves, (A)nd if we think them not enlightened enough to exercise their control with a wholesome discretion, the remedy is not to take it from them, but to inform their discretion by education. This is the true corrective of abuses of constitutional power."
- Thomas Jefferson

"It takes time to persuade men to do even what is for their own good." **- Thomas Jefferson**

We can no longer refrain from engaging others in our Constitution-based, *limited government* point of view. Only when the centralization of power and money with the *political elite's Big Government* is again decentralized, as intended by our *Founding Fathers*, will our freedoms and liberties be guaranteed. As discussed in Chapter 7 on *Freedom of Speech*, speaking out and educating others is our only means to overcome the *political elite's* use of saturation and *Political Correctness* to espouse and enforce their point of view. Saturation is accomplished through repetition and coordinated talking points in collaboration with the complicit education system and *elite* media.

Instead of simply providing logical arguments, we must learn to engage both the hearts and minds of listeners by making connections to their pre-existing beliefs and using moral arguments. Those advocating for *Big Government* shroud all of their issues or arguments in "moral garments" such as *fairness, Social Justice, children's health*, and *saving the environment*. They also effectively use stories about real people to make their point and to engage the listeners' hearts. Too frequently, those who advocate for *limited government* use messages that are too detailed, insufficiently persuasive to the target audience, sound materialistic, and are perceived as preaching. Avoid rags to riches outlier stories. It is also important to communicate with people in a language that allows them to understand the issue. In other words, keep it simple. Start with a statement of moral purpose, i.e., state why you want to talk about something instead of what you want to talk about. Lastly, the message needs to be factual and non-inflammatory.

When discussing economic principles, as discussed later in this chapter, make sure to seize the moral high ground by articulating them in a context of compassion and fairness. Too often, those advocating for *limited government* sound too materialistic with their focus on taxes, debt, deficits, spending, and fiscal responsibility. Focus instead on improving all people's lives, especially those most vulnerable, affording them equal opportunities to earn success or make a living. This can be accomplished through education reform, skill development, private job creation, and entrepreneurship. Most people are dissatisfied with being given things to them for free, which robs them of their dignity and self-esteem, nor is such a system sustainable. Only through free enterprise, unencumbered by *Big Government's* onerous rules and regulations, can the poor have opportunities to become self-reliant and pursue happiness as guaranteed by our Constitution.

We also need to learn from those advocating for *Big Government* how to win arguments. While many misinformed and low-information constituents share a lot of the values and principles of the *Silent Majority*, they align themselves with the *political elite*'s ideas and arguments because they believe that the *political elite* are sophisticated and smart. In contrast, they have been told that those representing the *Silent Majority* are ignorant. We must change this perception by fighting back. We cannot expect to win by counter attacking with mere logic and facts. The misinformed and low-information constituents will be appalled when the *political elite*'s hypocrisy is exposed.

Furthermore, the *Silent Majority* needs to get the *political elite* to argue with themselves. In essence, the *Silent Majority* must argue a *political elite's* position with another *political elite's* position that contradicts it. Some examples of this are provided in subsequent paragraphs. Even though you are not likely to have the *political elite* admit that you won the argument, the misinformed or low-information constituents listening in will realize the contradictions and hypocrisy. That is okay since our objective is not to win the argument, but to win converts. This whole dynamic even works with biased reporters. By the way, debating and insisting on winning the argument generally turns people off. It is important to be positive and lighthearted.

Usually all it takes to expose a *political elite's* hypocrisy is to ask questions about obvious contradictions with regard to what they say versus what they stand for or what they do. For example, we need to point out the irony that while *political elite* use moral arguments as a basis for asserting improvements for the common good, they hold the belief that Judeo-Christian moral beliefs are purely a personal matter. Furthermore, the *political elite* frequently challenge the *Silent Majority* to live up to their Judeo-Christian values and principles, knowing full well that *people of faith* recognize that everyone sins and thus cannot live up to Christianity's moral teachings at all times. In contrast, since the *political elite* make no claims to any moral standards, they cannot be held similarly accountable. The *political elite* claim that *limited government* advocacy refers to Tenth Amendment states' rights, which they erroneously link to slavery, thereby suggesting that you might be for slavery. This accusation implies that *Big Government* is always right. We need to point out that *Big Government* was also wrong at one time with the Supreme Court's Dred Scott[83] decision in 1857 upholding slavery. However, in 2015, *Big Government* appears quite willing to advocate states' rights by allowing states to ignore federal immigration and marijuana laws. Such hypocrisy!

The *political elite* may preach tolerance of opinion and *freedom of speech*, but rarely practice it when it relates to opposing *Silent Majority* ideas. They will also state such things as "poverty is bad" and "the environment must be saved", while believing Darwin's evolution theory based on *survival of the fittest*. They believe, after all, that mankind is engaged in a meaningless struggle for survival. Other key value positions the *political elite* preach but do not practice are: "all morals are relative", "it is wrong to impose your values on someone else", "diversity is good", "we need strong women in society", "hate speech is bad", and "artistic standards are a matter of personal preference".

The most effective verbal weapon the *Silent Majority* can use is satire and ridicule, e.g., solving the debt crisis by borrowing money. Much that is tolerated through humor would be rejected if presented seriously. Humor works because it is impossible to counterattack ridicule. It infuriates the opposition and frequently causes the opposition to make foolish missteps. Cartoons can also be very effective. Through humor, we can expose the fact that *political elite* thinking frequently is at odds with itself and with common sense. Or through humor, we can create the impression that *political elite* thinking is odd and incongruent with *Silent Majority* thinking. When the *political elite* sense that they are not taken seriously, and instead are viewed as humorous, they will lose confidence, their arrogance, and their will to fight.

Many laws, rules, and regulations created by *political elite* government bureaucracies are internally inconsistent, defy common sense, and can thus be used against them in arguments to make a point. Stated differently, a citizen who follows a given law, rule, or regulation could, at the same time, be violating another law, rule, or regulation. We need to undermine the *political elite's* arrogance and confidence with doubt, hesitation, and embarrassment. This technique works well with low-information voters who are typically not interested in politics and are cynical about both political parties. Low-information voters normally react negatively to threats to their personal resources, freedoms, and any unfairness of laws, rules, or regulations.

Misinformed voters, on the other hand, are more interested in politics and view themselves as well-informed, although they are typically indoctrinated by *political elite* biased media outlets. A confrontational approach with them will likely backfire, although they can be persuaded by arguments pertaining to any laws, rules, and regulations that can be exposed as being unfair, that actually hurt those they claim to help, or that can be exposed as actually hurting the country. With misinformed voters, it is usually most effective to expand the discussion from narrow, practical considerations to a discussion of underlying deeper principles, where the *political elite's* ideology usually falls apart. Emphasize the distance between the *political elite's* positions and those of the *Silent Majority*, e.g., on issues such as spending, tax barriers to jobs, and homeland security.

Beware that the *political elite* frequently frame their arguments by making assumptions, at times using "straw men", and then focusing their arguments on very narrow topics. To counter this, expose the incorrect underlying assumptions. When the *political elite* are forced to defend, they either change the narrative or agree that both sides are guilty of the accusations. Should they play the *race card*, counter with how much damage their policies have done to the black family and their communities. Never criticize teachers, but instead focus on how the *Teacher Unions* hide their agenda behind innocent children in schools and raise money for *political elite Big Government* politicians. Another favorite tactic is to quickly morph themselves into a victim when attacked. To counter this, the *Silent Majority* needs to hit hard and then quickly seize the moral high ground by calling for an end to all negativity.

Some of the key points discussed in this section are gleaned from an excellent book, *Waking the Sleeping Giant:*

How Mainstream Americans Can Beat Liberals at Their Own Game, written by psychologists Timothy C. Daughtry and Gary R. Casselman. I encourage you to buy this outstanding book and read it. It has much more extensive perspective and content than is shared here.

Economics 101

Our well-being is very much linked to the nation's economy. Therefore, it is of utmost importance that we obtain truthful perspective about the economy's status and that everyone has a correct understanding of economic principles. This ensures that we advocate and support correct government measures to stimulate growth and the welfare of all constituents. With this in mind, I provide two contrasting economic perspectives, one as viewed by those advocating an all-powerful *Big Government*[84] and the other based on a proper understanding of economics. I do this to assist your actions and advocacy as discussed in this chapter. In essence, many "unintended consequences" of government policies can easily be prevented with a better understanding of economic principles. *Political elite*, and many well-intentioned people, all too often focus on what is *seen* in economics but are clueless about what is *not seen*, such as how minimum wages destroy jobs. Using this line of reasoning, theologians have no business discussing economics unless they have studied it.

As an example, I am reminded of a fictional story in which a *Silent Majority* neighbor with two cars lives next to a *Big Government* aligned neighbor with one car, who in turn has an unemployed neighbor with no cars. The neighbor with no cars tells the *Big Government* aligned neighbor that he could use a car so that he can find employment. The latter contacts *Big Government* officials and suggests taking one car from the *Silent Majority* neighbor with two cars and giving it to his neighbor with no cars. The *Big Government* officials agree that this would be *Social Justice* and facilitate the transfer of cars. Now everyone is equal and every neighbor has just one car. The *Big Government* officials feel great about having done what is fair, the *Big Government* aligned neighbor feels great about having brought this unfair situation to the officials' attention, and the unemployed neighbor feels great about having received a car. The *Silent Majority* neighbor, however, is quite upset about having lost one of his cars for which he and his wife had worked multiple jobs and sacrificed much. But he is helpless to do anything since he is in the minority, i.e., only one of four who feels bad about the situation. He and his wife decide that from now on, since protesting is futile, they will no longer work so hard and sacrifice so much. Instead, they too will rely on *Social Justice* for their welfare. The actions of the *Silent Majority* couple are totally out of sight from the public, while the other neighbors' actions are seen by the public and are reported in the news as having been virtuous. This is an excellent supply-side economics example, i.e., if you make something more attractive (e.g., welfare), you get more of it; if you make it less attractive (e.g., work), you get less.

It should be noted that wealth and a higher standard of living can only be created when productivity (value produced per person-hour) is increased through innovation or leverage of technology, not by transferring wealth in a zero-sum manner. New technology can only be achieved through investments. Furthermore, the productivity of labor determines the supply of consumer goods relative to the supply of labor, and thus determines the prices of consumer goods relative to wage rates. Net, only through productivity are wages raised, wealth created, and standard of living improved. You should be aware that many *elite politicians* who believe in *Big Government* do not view investments and financial markets to be part of the economy. Instead, they view these as part of a fictitious, imaginary economy[85]. Net, they do not value the concept of risk, where capital is raised to build business infrastructure, e.g., buildings and equipment. The risk is taken based on an entrepreneur's belief that a demand exists for the planned products or services. This same flaw exists in Karl Marx's logic as he espouses Communism in his book, *Communist Manifesto*. Marx did not factor a return-on-investment for risk into his calculations to determine how much workers should be paid based on a product's retail price.

Government spending or increase of the money supply through *Quantitative Easing* (the Federal Reserve prints money and loans it to the Treasury in exchange for bonds) cannot achieve productivity improvements and thus cannot improve the standard of living. Instead, they result in inflation. Government is only an intermediary that transfers money from the broad-based private sector to those it selects as winners. It does not have a profit/productivity improvement motive and is only concerned with collecting taxes to fund its operations, redistributing money to political allies, national defense, and enforcing rules and regulations. *Big Government* advocates believe that we need to *"boost growth in an ecologically sustainable manner, which only massive government intervention can achieve"*[86]. They deride the *Silent Majority* for feeling that *"if we spend tomorrow's money today, we won't have it tomorrow. Our children won't have it."*[87] Instead, they mistakenly feel that creating government debt *"can lead to having far more money tomorrow. A good loan pays for itself."*[88]

Money facilitates exchange of goods and services and eliminates the need for barter, in which two people with two disparate needs must find each other and agree on exchange quantities. Prices based on money and profits provide feedback signals to companies to assure them that their products or services are correctly priced for their market and that they have employed resources in conformity with consumer desires. Prices are determined by market-based supply-and-demand, facilitate proper allocation of scarce resources, and provide incentives during shortages for others to get into the business. Price controls ignore these market-based realities and typically result in shortages, long lines, and generally poor customer service.

Wages are based on money and facilitate employment of people with dissimilar skills and interests. The amount of each wage is determined by the supply-and-demand of these skills in the market. Any artificial manipulation to increase wages will lead to subsequent losses in jobs since businesses must maintain competitive operating costs. For example, minimum wage laws or higher wages obtained through collective union bargaining lead to job losses. Everyone sees the immediate benefits of higher wages for the affected workers, but no one sees the associated job losses.

Our current high unemployment is a moral outrage. It is hurting the poor the most and is creating unnecessary dependencies on government. While the employment level in 2013 was 62.8%, the lowest in almost four decades[89], the employment of 16-24 year olds, who are most affected by minimum wage requirements, dropped from 61.6% in 2003 to 55% in 2013[90]. Unemployment among black youths is the worst with 40% unemployed[91]. Despite all of these dismal economic factors, politicians of both parties and big business, by way of the U.S. Chamber of Commerce, want to increase the labor pool with low wage labor through immigration reform. It should not be a mystery whose interests these *elite politicians* are looking out for.

Importantly, none of the above economic principles apply to government workers since the government has monopolistic powers. It can either seize more "revenue" from its citizens through taxation to pay for ever-increasing operating costs, or simply print more money. Without pricing and profit feedback signals from the market, government allocation of resources has no basis other than the beliefs of central planners.

Consequently, the government operates inefficiently and wastefully. Ask yourself why your shopping experience at UPS, FedEx, Office Depot, Target, etc. differs so greatly from the government-run Post Office, License Bureau, etc.? As stated above, lack of market-based feedback results in shortages, long lines, and generally poor customer service.

Some of the key economic principles discussed in this section are gleaned from an excellent book, *The Church And The Market*, by Thomas E. Woods Jr.. Despite the title, this book is an easy-to-read economics book rather than a religious book. I consider it to be one of the better economics books for lay people.

---

[83] Wikipedia, *Dred Scott v. Sandford*, The Free Encyclopedia, https://en.wikipedia.org/wiki/Dred_Scott_v._Sandford (November 7, 2015).

[84] Max & Kendall Bobo, *Organizing for Social Change*, 4th Edition (Santa Ana, CA: The Forum Press, 2010), 365 – 366.

[85] Bobo, 366.

[86] Bobo, 373.

[87] Bobo, 374.

[88] Bobo, 374.

[89] Ali Meyer, *62.8%: Labor Force Participation Has Hovered Near 37-Year-Low for 11 Months*, CNS News, http://www.cnsnews.com/news/article/ali-meyer/628-labor-force-participation-has-hovered-near-37-year-low-11-months (March 6, 2015).

[90] Ben Casselman, *Number of the Week: Fewer Than Half of Young People Will Be in Work Force*, Wall Street Journal, http://blogs.wsj.com/economics/2013/12/21/number-of-the-week-fewer-than-half-of-young-people-will-be-in-work-force/ (December 21, 2013).

[91] Daniel Boffey, *Youth unemployment rate is worst for 20 years, compared with overall figure: 16-24-year-olds are three times as likely to be jobless*, The Guardian, http://www.theguardian.com/society/2015/feb/22/youth-unemployment-jobless-figure (February 21, 2015).

Chapter 10

=================

Outreach – Neighborly Love

"A nation of well-informed men who have been taught to know and prize the rights which God has given them cannot be enslaved. It is in the region of ignorance that tyranny begins." - **Ben Franklin**

"The advancement and diffusion of knowledge is the only guardian of true liberty." - **James Madison**

"America will never be destroyed from the outside. If we falter and lose our freedoms, it will be because we destroyed ourselves."
- **Abraham Lincoln**

We must avoid self-segregation with like-minded folks and reach out to others to enlighten and educate them to the realities of our common predicament and inform them why it is incumbent on us to work together. This can be done one-on-one or at the *Neighborhood Meeting* group level. We must become "missionaries" for the *Silent Majority* and through humility, courage, and clarity of purpose cause others to realize that they are either already one of us or that they too want to share in our vision for America. Walk among others, learn what motivates them, ask questions, and dare them to think differently. But do not be an ideologue. Your objective is to find common ground and win over persuadable Americans so that they too want to partake in the *American Dream* pursued by the *Silent Majority*. Only by reaching out and engaging hearts and minds will we regain the powers entrusted in us, *We the People,* by our *Founding Fathers*.

It is ironic that the *political elite* often cite that *"it takes a village"*, when in fact, they attempt to divide us. Much of their focus is on isolating us from each other by *Balkanizing* us into special interest groups. They do this by pandering solutions to each group that only *Big Government* can provide. For example, one of the *political elite's* communication strategy documents states, *"Targeting and segmentation are crucial to breaking through and having the edge to persuade.... Once identified, figure out how to reach them via their belief system and common ground. It's easier to motivate someone around something they already believe than to convince them of something new.*[92]*"* Ironically, they advocate these issues and solutions despite hurting the overall common good. The consequence is that since, as they say, *"...divided we fall"*, *Big Government* and their affiliated big businesses and institutions have all the power and *We the People* are powerless. Everyone must be made aware of their agenda and be mobilized to do something about it.

To succeed, we must focus on what we have in common, such as faith, values, principles, morals, and focus on the family, instead of what may divide us, such as solutions to specific issues. Stated differently, by focusing on the overall vision for our communities and country instead of specific issues, you will find much common ground. You will be most effective if you start your conversations with an explicit moral focus and a focus on fighting for people. By appealing to compassion and fairness, you will engage the hearts and minds of persuadable listeners. It is not so important to have talking points, but instead, for people to see that those who advocate for *limited government* are friendly and share many of their own beliefs, despite what others may have told them. Nevertheless, remember, first impressions are made in less than half a minute and you generally do not get a second chance. Consequently, make eye contact, have an authentic smile, and concisely state what animates *Silent Majority* hearts. You will be amazed at how much more we have in common, instead of what may divide us.

I am reminded of a success example of this outreach approach from the Los Angeles area *Pasadena Patriots*[93], who successfully engaged predominantly African-American and Hispanic communities. I met their leader in 2010 at the first *National Tea Party Convention* in Nashville. In subsequent phone conversations, he enthusiastically shared with me their success in engaging minorities and having them join their movement. He also was kind enough to provide feedback on how well my *Neighborhood Organizing* presentation on *Getting-Out-The-Vote*, as discussed in Chapter 14, was received by his other leaders and organization members. As a testimonial to their success, *Human Events* published an article titled, *"'Dose of Tea' Brings New Life to Los Angeles GOP"*[94].

People of Faith

We should also be able to engage *people of faith* and faith communities since they are under assault by the *political elite* and *Big Government* for practicing their faith in the *public square*. Faith communities represent established organizations with established relationships among members who can be quickly mobilized. Unfortunately, many religious leaders recognize that they are at war but are afraid to become engaged due to unfounded 501(c)(3) concerns, thus encumbering any civic or political involvement of their membership. In reality, the only constraint a nonpartisan 501(c)(3) status provides is that churches are prohibited from endorsing specific candidates. It should be noted that due to the assault on religious freedom by the *political elite* and *Big Government*, many church members previously aligned with the *political elite* are now questioning their allegiances, e.g., African-American pastors, embarrassed liberal Catholics, and staunch Catholic Hispanics.

Consequently, while we should engage church leadership, we must also find members within these church communities who are concerned about religious freedom and who are willing to put their faith into action. This can be accomplished by contacting church groups and hosting *Neighborhood Meetings* for concerned church members. In other words, work from both the top down and the bottom up. We have already become aware of a few success examples. One is where a *person of faith* in Long Island, New York spoke at a rally about *freedom of religion*. In response, about fifty people from various parishes offered to help fight for religious freedom. Knoxville, TN groups had success by just having a few people stand outside of Catholic churches with signs indicating that they support the Catholic Church and its pursuit of religious freedom. As a result, many parishioners offered to help the fight for religious freedom and even priests thanked these groups for their initiative.

Small and Mid-Sized Businesses

Small and mid-sized businesses can also be approached by *Neighborhood Meeting* groups as allies against the *political elite's Big Government* agenda. They can help with funding strategies and tactics. This can be a synergistic relationship since grassroots citizen groups do not have much money while small and mid-sized business owners do not have much time. Clearly, the *political elite's* policies on behalf of *Big Government*, *big labor*, and big business, with their many taxes, rules, and regulations, are destructive to small and mid-sized businesses. Many congressional bills only provide guidance while relying on the various federal agencies, with help from big business lobbyists, to create the detailed rules and regulations. Large businesses have the resources to influence rules and regulations to favor themselves, while small and mid-sized businesses do not. Once these local small and mid-sized businesses disappear, big businesses will fill the void with their branch operations.

Up to now, small and mid-sized businesses have relied on organizations such as *The Chamber of Commerce*, the *National Small Business Association*, *U.S. Small Business Administration*, and *The Business Roundtable* to represent and advocate their interests. Unfortunately, these organizations have either misjudged their deal-making or have been ineffective in their lobbying to stop the current assault on small and mid-sized businesses. Small and mid-sized businesses' only recourse now is to align themselves with local nonpartisan citizen groups focused on leveraging their large base of informed and passionate citizens to advocate and fight for the principles of *limited government, free markets*, and *individual liberties*. Only with adherence to these constitutional principles can small and mid-sized businesses continue to prosper in our uniquely American capitalistic system.

Small and mid-sized businesses can learn from the *political elite's Big Government* playbook, *THE BLUEPRINT – How the Democrats Won Colorado*, written in 2010 by Adam Schrager and Rob Witwer. The book describes an innovative donor model in which businesses direct contributions to aligned local citizen groups, each of which provides different and complementary capabilities. This distributed network of aligned local groups limits transparency, minimizes duplicative efforts, completely hides the flow of donor money, and insulates the network from missteps by any of the aligned local groups. Importantly, this donor model ensures efficient and effective utilization of donor money without an intermediary entity or organization that can enrich itself first and then direct the remaining funds to its favored initiatives.

---

[92] Kristen Wolf, *NOW HEAR THIS - THE NINE LAWS OF SUCCESSFUL ADVOCACY COMMUNICATIONS*, Fenton Communications, http://www.beyondpesticides.org/assets/media/documents/how-to/media/Packard_Brochure.pdf (November 7, 2015).

[93] The Pasadena Patriots, http://www.teapac.net/TP_PROD/ (November 7, 2015).

[94] John Gizzi, *"Dose of Tea" Brings New Life to Los Angeles GOP, Human Events*, Human Events, http://humanevents.com/2010/08/21/dose-of-tea-brings-new-life-to-los-angeles-gop/ (August 21, 2010).

Chapter 11

==================

Politics – Take Back Your Government

"The people are responsible for the character of their Congress. If that body be ignorant, reckless, and corrupt, it is because the people tolerate ignorance, recklessness, and corruption. If it be intelligent, brave, and pure, it is because the people demand these high qualities. ... If the next centennial does not find us a great nation ...it will be because those who represent the enterprise, the culture, and the morality of the nation do not aid in controlling the political forces."

- Rev. James A. Garfield (1831-1881), United States President

"Patriotism means to stand by the country. It does NOT mean to stand by the President or any other public official save exactly to the degree in which he himself stands by the country. It is patriotic to support him insofar as he efficiently serves the country. It is unpatriotic not to oppose him to the exact extent that by inefficiency or otherwise he fails in his duty to stand by the country." **- Theodore Roosevelt**

America's *Founding Fathers* were very much for individuals exercising their civic duties and were against political parties. Our *Founding Fathers* placed principles over party; went to Congress to serve, not to be served; sought common ground; and passed laws with the knowledge that they would have to return home to live under those laws. With regard to political parties, John Adams commented, *"There is nothing which I dread so much as a division of the republic into two great parties, each arranged under its leader, and concerting measures in opposition to each other. This, in my humble apprehension, is to be dreaded as the greatest political evil under our Constitution."*[95] This is precisely where we find ourselves today, i.e., *elite politicians* no longer represent their constituent voters and instead, are loyal to their party and its aligned big businesses and institutions.

Just because we, the *Silent Majority* constituents, have awakened to the fact that we have become victims of the *elite politicians* and *Big Government*, do not for a second believe that changing this situation will be easy! The *elites* will do everything they can to maintain their status and power. Politicians of both parties have created laws and regulations that make it very difficult for them to be challenged politically in elections by anyone outside the *Establishment* of their party. In

Ohio, for example, if a challenger loses a primary election to a party *elite politician*, he/she is not able to run as an independent for any office except school board in the general election. This is due to Ohio's *Sore Loser Law* passed by *elite politicians*. Even within parties, the *elites* have changed rules and bylaws as needed to prevent *limited government* advocates from having any influence in selecting party candidates. In 2012, GOP party conventions in Missouri, Arizona, Oklahoma, Louisiana, and other states erupted in chaos when *limited government* leaning attendees protested rule changes.[96]

Elite politicians, together with a complicit *elite* mainstream media, have vilified private citizens who are concerned about out-of-control *Big Government,* called them racists, and accused them of being funded by wealthy individuals. While these accusations are patently unfounded, they are unfortunately believed by much of the public. The IRS actively targeted *limited government* oriented nonprofit organizations in the run-up to the 2012 election to mitigate their influence[97]. In 2014, even while denying these allegations, the IRS attempted to codify this behavior with rules that prevented *limited government* oriented organizations from participating in politics[98]. The brashness of these attempts by *elite politicians* and *Big Government* bureaucrats to stop common citizens from getting involved in politics is mind-boggling!

I can personally relate to this type of resistance to change that threatens an existing power structure. For the last ten years of my corporate career, I was a change agent with broad authority to change work processes in order to make them more effective and efficient. Fortunately, I had high level corporate executive protection. On a number of occasions, however, when my ideas threatened the power and budgets of other high level executives, they tried to have me fired by using creative pretenses. The point is that no change will occur until you, the *Silent Majority,* gets actively involved and demands change.

Precinct Executive / Central Committee

Constituents who believe in the constitutional principles of *limited government, free markets*, and *individual liberties* may want to join the local party organizations, either Democrat or Republican, in order to affect party policy and candidate selection. Any individual can apply to be his/her party's precinct representative on the party's *Central Committee.* All you need to do is complete a petition from your local *Board of Elections* and campaign in your neighborhood precinct using the *Get-Out-The-Vote* best practices discussed in Chapter 14. You may also want to solicit help from your neighboring liberty-minded organizations, get yourself on the liberty-minded organizations' *Voter Guides*, and encourage independents to declare a party during the primary or caucus election and vote for you. Many of the local Precinct Executive/*County Central Committee* positions are vacant and 30-50% of the time you may actually run unopposed.

Laws and rules for petition applications vary by state, and potentially by county, requiring that you check with your local *Board of Elections* to completely and thoroughly understand the laws and rules to ensure that your petition is not disqualified. Experience has shown that incumbent *Big Government* career politicians are anxious to disqualify any *limited government* candidate's petition based on the smallest technicalities. For example, to apply to run for Precinct Executive/*County Central Committee* in Ohio, an applicant needs valid signatures of at least five registered voters who are registered in the same party as the applicant. In 2012, the petition form provided lines for fifteen signatures. If you submitted the petition with more than fifteen signatures, however, the petition was disqualified. So beware and know all of the requirements and make sure you know the date petitions must be returned to the *Board of Elections* prior to the primary election.

As an advocate of *limited government, free markets,* and *individual liberties,* expect resistance from the incumbent *Big Government* career politicians when you decide to run for your party's precinct representative position. In the 2010 primary election, the Ohio GOP spent over a million dollars to defeat *limited government* oriented Precinct Executive/*County Central Committee* candidates to ensure that their party's favored candidates were elected. They did this despite internal party rules prohibiting candidate advocacy for party Precinct Executive/*County Central Committee* elections. Nevertheless, many *limited government* candidates won.

Make sure that you are applying to run for the proper position within the party to fully realize your goal of affecting party policy and candidate selection. In many states, the parties have a two-tiered system of Precinct Executive/*County Central Committee* and *State Central Committee,* with the latter having most of the power within a state and with the national party organization. While the Precinct Executive/*County Central Committee* representatives are elected locally in neighborhood precincts, *State Central Committee* representatives are often elected on a state senate or legislative district basis. The latter is clearly more challenging and thus further protects the party's incumbent power structure.

Constituent Town Halls
With Elected Officials/Candidates

Neighborhood Meeting groups or organizations can sponsor *Constituent Town Halls* to allow constituents to either: 1) ask government official(s) questions, or 2) learn more about candidates prior to an election. These *Constituent Town Hall* events establish your group or organization as a force/authority in the community to be reckoned with. It makes sense to collaborate with local, like-minded *Neighborhood Meeting* groups or organizations to plan and execute a resource-intensive event such as a *Constituent Town Hall*. Most likely you are already aware of like-minded *Neighborhood Meeting* groups or organizations in your area, but you might want to check with your members and search the Internet to ensure that all organizations are provided the opportunity to participate. If you are planning to host election candidates, make sure that one of these groups or organizations has a 501(c)(3) or 501(c)(4) nonprofit status under which you can conduct the nonpartisan *Constituent Town Hall*.

You need to first identify which elected government official(s) or candidates to invite to the *Constituent Town Hall*. Nonprofit organizations are obliged to extend invitations, without bias, to all viable election candidates. To identify which election candidates are viable, determine who has registered with the *Federal Election Commission* or the *Board of Elections* in your voting district's most populous county. Once identified, contact the elected government official(s) or candidates and invite them to the *Constituent Town Hall*. While initial invitations can be informal, i.e., verbal, phone call, or e-mail, make sure the final invitations, with all relevant details, are sent to the elected government official(s) or candidates via registered mail. Request a written response, either via e-mail or U.S. Mail. Indicate that unless the elected government official or candidate has a verifiable, valid reason for not attending the *Constituent Town Hall,* a seat will be reserved for him/her at the event and a prominently displayed name plate will be in front of the empty seat, all captured on video that will be accessible on the website. If an elected official declines to attend, have his/her political opponent(s) or a panel of knowledgeable "experts" field questions. All these incentives usually work.

Instead of having access to the questions beforehand, *Constituent Town Halls* are unscripted in that audience members' questions are random and broad-ranging. Make sure *Constituent Town Halls* occur well before voters receive their mail-in/absentee ballots, are videotaped, and are posted on a voter accessible website. Content from these *Constituent Town Halls* can be used in subsequent communications with constituents. Prior to elections, content can be incorporated in *Voter Guides* that can be distributed inexpensively via newspaper inserts or *Get-Out-The-Vote* canvassing. On Election Day, *Voter Guides* can be distributed near polling locations.

Constituent Town Hall PRE-WORK

- **Scope & Dates** – Select the date and decide which elected government official(s) or candidates to invite.
- **Organization** – Designate one individual for each of the following roles:
  1. Communications with elected government official(s) or candidates
  2. Secure venue & security
  3. Moderator for *Constituent Town Hall*, either from within the *limited government* groups/organizations or from outside, such as a local talk show host
  4. Individual or committee to interact with the press and handle press releases

5. Videotaping the event

6. Scorekeeper and note taker during the event

7. Audience microphone holder *(never leave a live mike unattended)*

8. Website design and upkeep

- **Venue** – Ensure the selected location is centralized and has sufficient seating for the anticipated turnout, although you want to make sure your anticipated attendance can come close to overfilling the venue. The nonprofit status will be beneficial in accessing local venues such as colleges, school auditoriums, churches, etc. Most likely you will be requested to sign a rental contract. You may want to purchase event liability insurance, since most likely the contract will state that your organization is responsible for damages, etc. Secure appropriate sound system capabilities and sufficient microphones for all elected government official(s) or candidates attending, the moderator, and two cordless microphones for audience questions.

- **Security** – Hire local police for this task. The venue provider may waive liability insurance requirements if you hire appropriate event security.

- **Website** – Create a website so that those constituents who could not attend the *Constituent Town Hall* can view the video in its entirety. Make sure you are explicit in stating that the video is copyrighted and that it cannot be used in its entirety, or portions thereof, unless approved by your group or organization, since candidates will be tempted to extract favorable clips of themselves and unfavorable portions of their opponents. Additionally, this website can be a repository for sharing straw poll results, relevant local *Voter Guides*, media coverage links, press releases, etc.

- **Publicity** – Ensure press releases are appropriately vetted by your group or organization prior to release - no later than one week prior to the event. Expect that initially the media will be slow to publicize your events, but they will come around. Phone all media assignment editors and producers (city desk, day books, bloggers, and wire services) the night prior to the event. Supplement press releases to the print media with appearances on local radio talk shows and by distributing and posting *Constituent Town Hall* flyers. Use your group or organization members to help get the word out. Announce the event at other community events. Plan to use phone banks or robocalls to call liberty-oriented constituents several times prior to the event. In your calls, stress the common *limited government* orientation, importance of the event, previous successes, their role in asking questions, and that a good turnout is important. Ask for a definite commitment to come. Lastly, you can inform constituents via a leaflet-drop in a door-to-door canvass.

- **Funding** – Cover out-of-pocket *Constituent Town Hall* expenses by seeking local donations from individuals, groups, businesses, and by collecting donations at the event. Bring wrapped cans or containers to the event for collections. *Limited government* advocates tend to be fairly generous in supporting grassroots efforts.

Constituent Town Hall LOGISTICS

- **Event Length** - Plan on a three to four-hour event, with maybe a fifteen-minute break halfway. Experience has shown that attendees are even willing to extend the allocated time as they become engaged in the event.

- **As Audience Arrives** – When audience members enter the *Constituent Town Hall* event, ask if they would like to ask a question. Give them a card to fill out with their name. Retain the card for random selection of questioners. You may also want to distribute straw poll pamphlets to be collected at the conclusion of the *Constituent Town Hall*, to tally if minds were changed, interest in the event, and to rank the three top candidates, if present prior to an election.

Importantly, have ushers direct all arriving attendees to a staffed table for registration to obtain relevant contact information such as name, address, e-mail, and phone number.

- **Event Organizer** – Introduces self, *Pledge of Allegiance*, prayer, welcome, background on *Constituent Town Hall*, asks for donations, and introduces moderator.

- **Moderator**

  1. Welcome and introduction of elected official(s) or candidates by reading a provided short BIO - may have to be abbreviated.

  2. Each elected official or candidate gets 3-5 minutes to provide an introductory statement. Candidates can include why they are seeking the elected office.

  3. Explain all rules as outlined below. Encourage audience members to submit additional questions once the discussion starts. Experience has shown that audience members get very motivated to ask more questions once the elected official(s) or candidates start talking.

  4. Maintain control of event, but be somewhat flexible. Too much control or "tyrannical" behavior will cause the audience to sympathize with those being questioned.

- **Audience Questions**
  1. Use a timekeeper to time audience member questions and responses from elected officials(s) or candidates. Have timekeeper hold up "*1 Minute Left*" and "*Time Is Up*" signs, as appropriate.
  2. Randomly select questioner cards and announce who will get to ask question. Bring portable microphone to audience member with question.
  3. Audience members have 30 seconds to ask a question. They can either: 1) ask one question of one elected official or candidate, who has three minutes to answer, with an optional audience member follow-up question, for which the elected official or candidate has one minute to respond, or 2) ask a single question of more than one elected official or candidate, all of whom have one minute each to respond, with no audience member follow-up questions.
  4. Only questions are allowed, no statements.
  5. "Yes" or "No" questions must be answered with a "Yes" or "No" by elected official(s) or candidates, with an allowed three-minute follow-up to explain his/her position.

- **Elected official or candidate Closing Statements** – If time permits, each elected official or candidate gets 2-3 minutes for a closing statement.

- **Wrap-Up** - Thank everyone, request donations, request that they drop off straw poll pamphlets and direct everyone to your group's or organization's website for event video, straw poll results, and *Constituent Town Hall* discussion key points.

I want to thank Dan W. Offineer, who personally spent much time and effort in capturing many of the above-shared best practices. He was the *Candidate Night* Project Coordinator for Ohio District 18 in 2010. His efforts were rewarded with much praise from attendees and local media for having conducted an effective and unbiased *Candidate Night*.

---

[95] Steve Staub, *John Adams, Letter to Jonathan Jackson, October 1780*, The Federalist Papers Project, https://www.thefederalistpapers.org/founders/adams/john-adams-letter-to-jonathan-jackson-october-1780 (November 7, 2015).

[96] Ben Schwann, *Truth in Media "End Partisanship,"* https://www.youtube.com/watch?v=h1zRfXkOmPI

---

97 Juliet Eilperin, Zachary A. Goldfarb, "IRS officials in Washington were involved in targeting of conservative groups", *The Washington Post*, May 13, 2013 (https://www.washingtonpost.com/politics/obama-denounces-reported-irs-targeting-of-conservative-groups/2013/05/13/a0185644-bbdf-11e2-97d4-a479289a31f9_story.html).

98 George F. Will, "The IRS has a one-sided interest in politics", *The Washington Post*, March 7, 2014 (https://www.washingtonpost.com/opinions/george-f-will-the-irs-has-a-one-sided-interest-in-politics/2014/03/07/a545366a-a56c-11e3-84d4-e59b1709222c_story.html).

Chapter 12

========================

Investigation – Fight Cronyism and Corruption

"Our country is now taking so steady a course as to show by what road it will pass to destruction, to wit: by consolidation of power first, and then corruption, its necessary consequence." **-Thomas Jefferson**

"I am a firm believer in the people. If given the truth, they can be depended upon to meet any national crisis. The great point is to bring them the real facts." **- Abraham Lincoln**

If we are to prevent a centralized consolidation of power and wealth in *Big Government* run by *political elites,* we must be vigilant of inappropriate influences from big businesses and institutions. They have much to gain from such powerful alliances at the expense of the American people. Investigations can uncover conflicts of interest, actions inconsistent with laws or regulations, or outright lies. Fortunately, you do not need to be an expert to be vigilant since much information is freely available online, available from government agencies, or can be obtained at your local library. Paid subscription services such as *Lexis-Nexis* and *Westlaw* are also available. Prior to pursuing an investigation, be sure that you know what likely actions you will take with uncovered information, consistent with your strategies and tactics as discussed in Chapter 4.

The *Midwest Academy's* manual for activists, *Organizing For Social Change*, does an excellent job of providing detailed instructions for pursuing tactical investigations. It is based on the work of the *Corporate Research Project of Good Jobs First*, which can be accessed for free at *http://corp-research.org/dddresearchguide*. Much of the information I share below is gleaned from these sources.

A good start would be to focus on lobbyists. They represent interests outside of government and have the most to gain from government laws and regulations, many times superseding the interests of constituents. Many former politicians or government employees become lobbyists, consultants, and strategists, which allows them to leverage their connections and friendships in the legislature while further enriching themselves. To investigate these "revolving door" politicians or government employees, see the *Open Secrets* website (*http://www.opensecrets.org/revolving/index.php)*. Companies have to report their lobbying expenditures and lobbyists they employ. Likewise, federal lobbyists have to report their income and clients semi-annually to both the Senate and the House of Representatives. A great lobbying database created by the *Center for Responsive Politics* is available from *Open Secrets* (*https://www.opensecrets.org/lobby/)*. The U.S. Senate makes all of its lobbying documents available on the Internet (*http://www.senate.gov/legislative/Public_Disclosure/ LDA_reports.htm)*. Go to *http://www.lobbyists.info/* for a subscription-based search website.

To assess government subsidies to companies, tax abatements/exemptions, or loan guarantees that companies may have secured from the federal government, check out the following entities and websites: *Commerce Department Advanced Technology Program NIST* (*http://www.atp.nist.gov/*) and the *Export-Import Bank* (*http://www.exim.gov/*), whose lapsed authority on July 1, 2015 could be reinstated. Unfortunately, only a limited number of states require that economic development subsidies be disclosed.

Based on Court of Appeals and U.S. Supreme Court rulings, companies, their executives, and unions can donate unlimited amounts of money to the many Super PACs, as long as the money does not directly go to individual campaigns. *Open Secrets* (*http://www.opensecrets.org/*) has one of the best online accessible databases covering these donations. Other resource sites are the *Federal Election Commission* (*http://www.fec.gov/pindex.shtml*) and *Political Money Line* (*http://www.politicalmoneyline.com*). For donors to state politicians, consult the *National Institute On Money In State Politics* (*http://www.followthemoney.org/*).

Companies, their executives, and unions can also attempt to mask their politically-oriented contributions through 501(c)(4) nonprofit institutions who in turn impact politics through PACs, campaigns, and lobbying efforts. These nonprofits can do this as long as they are considered to be enhancing the "social welfare", which is a nebulously defined term by the IRS. The *Capital Research Center* (*http://capitalresearch.org*) does opposition research on entities who are opposed to the principles of individual liberty, a free market economy, and limited constitutional government. *Guide Star* (*http://www.guidestar.org/*) is the world's largest source of information on nonprofit organizations. The *Foundation Center* (*http://foundationcenter.org*), established in 1956, is a leading source of corporate and foundation philanthropy information worldwide. It maintains the most comprehensive database of grant-makers and their grants. *NOZASearch* (*https://www.nozasearch.com/*) is yet another searchable database of charitable donations.

Use of the *Freedom of Information Act (FOIA, pronounced "foya")* is yet another free and easy means to obtain governmental information and records that can include private sector company or nonprofit information. Some agencies may ignore your request until you cite the relevant FOIA laws or threaten legal action. In general, it is prudent to develop a healthy relationship with government agency staff, many of whom want to be helpful and care about their agency's mission. The *National Freedom of Information Coalition (http://www.nfoic.org/)* is a great resource for learning more about FOIA. A great resource for automatically generating federal FOIA requests is the *Reporters Committee for Freedom of the Press* website (*https://www.ifoia.org/#!/*). For state and local automatically-generated FOIA requests, use SPLC's website (*http://www.splc.org/page/lettergenerator#*). If agencies threaten to charge high fees for documents, seize the moral high ground and contact an elected official or the media to complain.

Chapter 13

================

Protests, Boycotts, and Demonstrations

"To sin by silence when they should protest makes cowards of men. ...We the People are the rightful masters of both Congress and the Courts - not to overthrow the Constitution, but to overthrow the men who pervert the Constitution." **- Abraham Lincoln**

"It is the duty of the patriot to protect his country from its government." **- Thomas Paine**

"Silence in the face of evil is itself evil: God will not hold us guiltless. Not to speak is to speak. Not to act is to act." **- Dietrich Bonhoeffer**

"The people are the only sure reliance for the preservation of our liberty." **- Thomas Jefferson**

There may come a time when none of the strategies and tactics discussed in the other chapters are sufficient for regaining our *We the People* power back from the *political elite's Big Government* and affiliated big businesses and institutions. Consequently, short of becoming serfs controlled by the centralized power and wealth in *Big Government*, we must resort to more disruptive strategies and tactics which require protests, boycotts, and demonstrations. We can create pivotal newsworthy resistance events that loudly proclaim our convictions and tug on people's hearts with passion and emotion. *Big Government* advocates do this all the time through *Community Organizers*. *Organizing for Action* (OFA) has trained more than 10,000 organizers, who in turn have trained more than two million youths in Saul Alinsky protest tactics.[99] They know that expressed, emotional outrage elevates the legitimacy of an argument. The biased *elite media* then saturates its news cycles with these protests, further legitimizing the protesters and their demands.

For best practices on nonviolent protests, boycotts, and demonstrations, we need to consult the world-renowned expert, Gene Sharp[100]. He is a retired professor of political science at the University of Massachusetts, Dartmouth and founder of the *Albert Einstein Institution*[101], a nonprofit organization dedicated to advancing the study of nonviolent action. While one of his excellent books, *From Dictatorship to Democracy*, may have helped citizens of countless countries create democracies from totalitarian regimes, it is just as helpful for those hoping to retain a democracy. A free PDF version is available online[102]. Based on his worldwide impact, Gene Sharp was nominated for the *Nobel Peace Prize* in 2009, 2012, 2013, and 2015[103]. I share relevant insights below, many gleaned from Gene Sharp's book.

Only through citizens' cooperation and submission can a government become powerful and oppressive. The government only has power over matters to the extent that we lack the strength to resist these powers. Withdrawal of cooperation and submission thus become powerful actions to reestablish *limited government*, liberty, and freedoms. Defiance is difficult for those in power to combat, aggravates weaknesses, can be dispersed or concentrated, and can lead to errors in judgment or actions by those in power. It can be psychological, social, or economic in nature. Initial actions, as warranted, can move from selective, targeted resistance to mass defiance. The targeted resistance can consist of low-risk, confidence-building actions, such as wearing similarly colored clothes, placing flowers at places of symbolic importance, five-minute halts of activity, several minutes of silence, student boycotts of classes, temporary sit-ins at important offices, or brief physical occupations.

The targeted resistance actions cited above can be escalated to one or more of the following: boycotts, which are more effective against businesses than against products; marches/parades with noise and signs, which can be fun, have great optics, and require no speakers; periodic mass demonstrations, but only if assured of large crowds and where passersby can feed the event; vigils; and strikes/picket lines. Be aware of infiltrators and provocateurs who may purposely incite actions that reflect badly on your movement. Yet other defiance acts are: being "sick" or "unable" to work, deliberately working more slowly, educating children at home instead of sending them to school, and hunger strikes. Communication with large audiences can be achieved through your movement's newspapers, leaflets, books, and through social media.

Throughout, it is important to remember the following key insights: Abandonment of fear of an oppressive government is a key element in destroying its power, leading to more limited centralized government. Over-reaction by those in power against clearly nonviolent actions will result in the movement gaining even more adherents to the cause and further weakening those in power. Secrecy is rooted in fear, will increase fear, and results in reducing the number of people involved. Heed the stated cautions regarding negotiations discussed in Chapter 4.

Remember that basic issues, such as religious principles, issues of human freedom, and the whole transformation of society from the constitutional republic designed by our *Founding Fathers* should not be compromised in negotiations. Lastly, remember that *"Freedom is not free!"*

Importantly, espouse the moral high ground at all times, proclaim that you are fighting for the majority's freedoms and civil rights, and gain alignment behind an agenda that unites. We can learn from the *Civil Rights Movement* in the fifties. It started as a rebellion with Rosa Park's 1955 bus ride, the 1960 black student sit-in at the Greensboro, NC Woolworth's, and the 1961 mixed racial group, *Freedom Riders*, on buses. Dr. Martin Luther King Jr. then seized the moral and majoritarian high ground by challenging the nation to abide by *The Declaration of Independence's* guaranteed *"unalienable rights"* of *"Life, Liberty, and the pursuit of Happiness"* for all men.

---

[99] Paul Sperry, *How Obama is bankrolling a nonstop protest against invented outrage,* New York Post, http://nypost.com/2015/11/14/how-obama-is-bankrolling-a-non-stop-protest-against-invented-outrage/ (November 14, 2015).

[100] Wikipedia, *Gene Sharp*, The Free Encyclopedia, https://en.wikipedia.org/wiki/Gene_Sharp, (November 7, 2015).

[101] Albert Einstein Institution, *Advance the worldwide study and strategic use of nonviolent action.* http://www.aeinstein.org/ (November 7, 2015).

[102] Gene Sharp, *From Dictatorship to Democracy: A Conceptual Framework for Liberation,* Fourth U.S. Edition, http://www.aeinstein.org/wp-content/uploads/2013/09/FDTD.pdf (May, 2010).

[103] https://en.wikipedia.org/wiki/Gene_Sharp.

Chapter 14

================

Get-Out-The-Vote

"A democracy will continue to exist up until the time that voters discover that they can vote themselves generous gifts from the public treasury. From that moment on, the majority always votes for the candidates who promise the most benefits from the public treasury, with the result that every democracy will finally collapse due to loose fiscal policy, which is always followed by a dictatorship."
-Alexander Fraser Tyler's *Cycle of Democracy*

"But a Constitution of Government once changed from Freedom, can never be restored. Liberty, once lost, is lost forever." **- John Adams**

Any individual, *Neighborhood Meeting* group, or organization can impact politics and policy by pursuing *Get-Out-The-Vote* best practices to elect candidates aligned with the constitutional principles of *limited government*. You do not have to be affiliated with a political party. *Get-Out-The-Vote* is effective because only thirty percent of eligible people vote in primary elections and only sixty percent vote in mid-term and general elections. Consequently, any effort to mobilize like-minded individuals in your neighborhood precinct to vote on Election Day will have an enormous impact. Make sure to do this in a nonpartisan fashion by encouraging voters in your neighborhood precinct to only vote for candidates who are aligned with your values and principles, without recommending specific candidates.

Individuals who voluntarily pursue neighborhood precinct *Get-Out-The-Vote* efforts can each generate 50-150 new votes. Experienced volunteers are only slightly more effective than newcomers. In contrast, paid professional precinct workers on average will deliver no more than 10-50 new votes, since they lack conviction. Robert A. Heinlein, who wrote *Take Back Your Government* in 1946 based on his own experience in politics, states: *"Remember at all times ...the votes are in the precincts. ... Club meetings are primarily to arouse and hold together your volunteers ...Rallies are for morale building primarily and secondarily for publicity. ...It isn't hard to get adherents to your cause. ...Volunteer campaigns should not cost much... Elections are not won with dollars."* In essence, the cumulative effect on policy and politics of having *limited government* oriented individuals, *Neighborhood Meeting* groups, or organizations pursue *Get-Out-The-Vote* efforts cannot be matched by big business lobbying or money.

This chapter shares *Get-Out-The-Vote* best practices based on much research, such as gleaned from *Take Back Your Government* by Robert Heinlein and *Get Out The Vote, Second Edition: How to Increase Voter Turnout*, written in 2008 by two Yale professors, Donald P. Green and Alan S. Gerber. Once you properly understand *Get-Out-The-Vote* best practices, you will appreciate just how easy and manageable the methodology is to pursue in your neighborhood precinct by any one individual, *Neighborhood Meeting* group, or organization. Topics covered in this chapter are: how do I get started, who to contact, what do I say, when to start, can others help me, what to do and not do, what impact will it have, and what aids can help me.

We created *TheVoicesOfAmerica.org* in 2009 to share *Get-Out-The-Vote* best practices with *limited government* oriented individuals and leaders throughout the nation. Based on many conversations over the years with practitioners from around the country, numerous feedback testimonials listed on our website, and use of these methods in my own neighborhood precinct, these *Get-Out-The-Vote* best practices have been validated to be extremely effective. Specifically, *Get-Out-The-Vote* efforts in my own neighborhood precinct increased the number of like-minded voters who went to the polls in 2010 by +32% relative to 2006. We were also directly involved in having *Get-Out-The-Vote* best practices methods used to successfully defeat three incumbent Congressional representatives in their state primaries or caucuses.

It is important to recognize that to win in your precinct only requires that your efforts surpass those of rival precinct organizations. A well-organized *Get-Out-The-Vote* effort will not only affect presidential elections, but can even more easily impact state and local elections. Most people seem to regard the office of President as the only one of importance and the presidential election every four years as the "main" election. Nothing could be further from the truth. The most important office in a democracy is the local city councilman/woman or selectman/woman. The most important election is the local caucus or primary, and so on up to the "major" offices and the "major" elections. "Minor" candidates have a way of becoming President. Chances are better than two to one that any future President will make his start in one of the minor local offices which the politically naive hold in contempt. Consequently, if you want to affect the destiny of our country, take over your own neighborhood precinct with your friends and elect local officials.

How Do I Get Started?

All that is required to *Get-Out-The-Vote* in your neighborhood precinct are some volunteers to go door-to-door with you, a walking list, a brief fifteen-second script, and door hanger/*Voter Guides*. In order to create the walking list, you need a *Precinct Map (see picture on right)* and *Voter Registration Records* 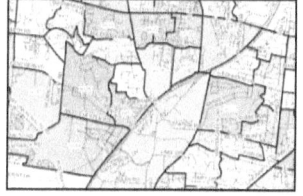 (with phone numbers, if available). Both are available from your county *Board of Elections,* either free or for a nominal fee. Many states and counties even have *Precinct Maps* and *Voter Registration Records* available on their websites. The *Voter Registration Records* are used to narrow the number of registered voters you need to contact to a more manageable number of voters, i.e., those who are most likely to be like-minded and willing to vote for the preferred candidates. Details on how to create this walking list are shared in the next section. A sample *Voter Registration Record* is shown on the next page.

LAST NAME	FIRST NAME	YEAR OF BIRTH	PARTY AFFILIATION	RESIDENTIAL ADDRESS	RESIDENTIAL CITY	RESIDENTIAL STATE	PRECINCT CODE	PRIMARY 03/04/2008	GENERAL 11/04/2008	PRIMARY 05/05/2009
		1989			MOUNT VERNON	OH	42AAK			
		1972	D		GAMBIER	OH	42AAX	D	X	X
		1971	D		GAMBIER	OH	42AAX	D	X	X
		1940	R		MOUNT VERNON	OH	42AAG	R	X	X
		1971			MOUNT VERNON	OH	42AAM		X	
		1967			GAMBIER	OH	42AAX			
		1940			MOUNT VERNON	OH	42AAJ		X	
		1946			MOUNT VERNON	OH	42AAJ		X	
		1922			MOUNT VERNON	OH	42AAM			
		1933	R		MOUNT VERNON	OH	42AAM	R	X	
		1984	R		MOUNT VERNON	OH	42AAJ	R	X	
		1976	R		FREDERICKTOWN	OH	42ACA	R	X	
		1979			FREDERICKTOWN	OH	42ACA		X	
		1955			MOUNT VERNON	OH	42AAJ			
		1915			MOUNT VERNON	OH	42AAE		X	
Name		1935		**Address**	MOUNT VERNON	OH	42AAE		X	
Blanked		1979		**Blanked**	MOUNT VERNON	OH	42AAA			
Out To		1966		**Out To**	CENTERBURG	OH	42AAZ		X	
Preserve		1920	D	**Preserve**	MOUNT VERNON	OH	42AAB			
Privacy		1924	D	**Privacy**	GAMBIER	OH	42AAX	D	X	
		1943			GAMBIER	OH	42AAX		X	X
		1939			GAMBIER	OH	42AAX		X	
		1976			GAMBIER	OH	42AAX			
		1979	R		MOUNT VERNON	OH	42AAG	R	X	
		1980	R		MOUNT VERNON	OH	42AAG	R	X	
		1935			GAMBIER	OH	42AAX		X	
		1939	D		GAMBIER	OH	42AAX		X	
		1965	D		MOUNT VERNON	OH	42AAA	D	X	X
		1926	R		MOUNT VERNON	OH	42ABL	R	X	X
		1948	R		MOUNT VERNON	OH	42AAC	R	X	
		1942	R		MOUNT VERNON	OH	42AAC	R	X	
		1985			MOUNT VERNON	OH	42AAA			
		1983			MOUNT VERNON	OH	42AAF			
		1932			MOUNT VERNON	OH	42AAG			
		1919	R		MOUNT VERNON	OH	42ABB		X	

The *Voter Registration Record* provides you with the names and addresses of all registered voters in your neighborhood precinct. Importantly, it shows "Party Affiliation" based on primary election participation and shows in which elections constituents voted.

If the *Voter Registration Record* is not already in Excel format, it will most likely be in a comma-delimited format that will need to be imported into an Excel program. Go to our website for detailed instructions on how to accomplish this (*http://thevoicesofamerica.org/Excel_Importation.html*). Focus only on *your* neighborhood precinct voter records by sorting the precinct code column in Excel and deleting all the other records.

Who To Contact?

Precincts on average have 1100 eligible voters, but the numbers vary across the country. Typically, of the eligible voters, 80% register to vote. Of all eligible voters, only about 60% actually vote in mid-term and general elections and fewer than 30% vote in primary elections. Consequently, it only takes 331 votes, on average, in a typical precinct to win a mid-term or general election. It only takes 83 votes, on average, to win a party's primary election, assuming a 50/50 split for the Democrat or Republican parties.

It is not necessary to contact all voters in a precinct in a *Get-Out-The-Vote* initiative. Assume that registered voters who always vote, as well as those who do not bother to vote, will continue to maintain their habits. This is regardless of party affiliation. Consequently, you can skip all the voters represented by black squares in the table on the right. You only target the voters represented by white squares.

Voter Turnout	Party Affiliation		
	Democrat	Independent	Republican
Always Vote	■	□	■
Sometimes Vote	■	□	□
Never Vote	■	■	■

These consist of independent voters who always and sometimes vote, since they may be swayed by the *limited government* message. Also include Republicans who sometimes vote, since they are likely to be *limited government* oriented but need encouragement to actually go and vote. With this focused approach, far fewer targeted voters need to be contacted in a neighborhood precinct to achieve the greater than 50% of actual votes needed to win. The *Voter Registration Record* will help determine into which square each neighborhood precinct voter belongs.

To demonstrate how important every neighborhood precinct vote is, note the following data. Democrats won the key pivotal states of Ohio and Minnesota in the 2008 presidential election with only ten additional Democrat voters per precinct. In 1976, Jimmy Carter won Ohio with an average of 1 vote advantage per precinct. George Bush, in 2000, won the Presidency with just 537 votes in Florida. As a further example of how a limited number of votes can win a precinct, note the grid below that is based on actual data from the *Voter Registration Records* of my own precinct in 2010.

	Avg. Eligible Voters Per Precinct	% Eligible Voters Registered	Registered Voters	Mid Term and General Elections	
				% Registered Voters Who Vote	Actual Voters
Butler County, OH - Precinct WC37					
Total	1000	86%	863	75%	647
Democrat			180	75%	135
Independent			382	75%	287
Republican			301	75%	226

The actual voter column on the right is where we need to focus. For one of the parties to win the precinct, it needs 324 votes.

A candidate would need less than 68 votes to win the Democrat primary, since far fewer voters show up during primary elections.

To create individual walking lists for each of your volunteers, create logical groupings of streets, or sections thereof, of 40 targeted households per volunteer. Do this in Excel by sorting the *Residential Address* column of the *Voter Registration Record* for your precinct. This will ensure that each volunteer is assigned a manageable number of households, since volunteers can cover about 20 households per hour with about 50% being home per trip. Volunteers will need to make multiple trips to reach everyone at home and talk to all of the targeted voters. To help with the logical groupings of streets, or sections thereof, use the *Precinct Map*.

What Do I Say?

You will most likely be successful in finding like-minded voters and ensure that they vote in elections by starting the conversation with targeted registered voters using the following brief message: *Hello: My name is _____ and I am a neighbor of yours. I am concerned that our government no longer represents us, but instead is rigged for the political elite, big businesses, and big institutions."* Polling shows that over eighty percent[104] of Americans across the board already believe this assertion. Next, encourage them to vote for all the candidates who are for *limited government, free markets,* and *individual freedoms,* without advocating for a specific candidate. At this point, you may choose to hand them a nonpartisan *Voter Guide,* discussed at the end of this chapter. Analyses show that strictly nonpartisan *Get-Out-The-Vote* efforts such as this are neither more nor less effective than campaigns organized around a specific candidate.

Many first-time volunteers have misconceptions that *Get-Out-The-Vote* efforts are analogous to making cold sales calls, i.e., where you have to convince an unreceptive customer to buy a product or service. Nothing could be further from the truth. In most likelihood, it will be a pleasant experience since all you are doing is looking for like-minded voters and making sure they go out and vote on Election Day. You already will have stacked the deck by creating a walking list of voters who are likely to be like-minded. Asking citizens if their vote can be counted on and providing them with mail-in voting and polling location information, including early voting locations, will further improve *Get-Out-The-Vote* turnout. Voters living at the same address also tend to mobilize each other.

Try to make a personal connection with your neighbors when you approach the door, based on observations such as kids' toys, presence of dogs, landscaping, political signs, etc. Stress that you are indeed a neighbor who voluntarily chose to do this and that you are not a professional political operative. Use your own personal story of why you chose to get involved. Listen to their concerns and validate their opinion as appropriate. Do not argue! Use simple language and be sincere, truthful, and genuine. End with a call for action such as voting or maybe joining your *Neighborhood Meeting* group in the precinct.

If a person is too busy, try to leave behind some nonpartisan reading material such as a door hanger or *Voter Guide*, discussed later in this chapter. If you are told that the person always votes party line, indicate that there is now dissention and therefore new candidate options exist within both parties. If you are told that their one vote is of no significance, share with them some of the data discussed above. If they state that all politicians are corrupt, affirm that one may indeed get this impression from the media and suggest that it is for this reason many good citizens are now choosing to run for office for the first time and that they will need his/her vote.

Importantly, a nonpartisan principle-based, simple message does not require that you form a *Political Action Committee* (PAC) with its many bookkeeping and filing requirements. In a meeting with lawyers from Ohio's Secretary of State's office, I was informed that a PAC or similar structure is necessary once a group of individuals or an organization *"are for or against a specific candidate and if money is involved"*. Even donating one's time and materials can be viewed as *in-kind contributions* to a candidate and require a PAC or similar legal entity. Laws in states may differ, so be sure to check with your Secretary of State. Furthermore, in contrast to partisan persuasive messaging for a specific candidate, which is only relevant for one campaign and has no long-term effect once the candidates move on, using nonpartisan constitutional principles of *limited government, free markets*, and *individual liberties* as a basis for selecting candidates has lasting relevance.

When To Start?

The first order of business is to ensure that all like-minded eligible voters are indeed registered to vote. Oftentimes, new neighbors who recently moved into the neighborhood forget to register in their new precinct. Frequently, eligible older children in households are not registered. If they are like-minded, give them a voter registration form so that they can register at least 30 days prior to Election Day.

With early voting and more pervasive mail-in balloting allowed in more states, it is imperative to engage voters accordingly in your neighborhood precinct. Obtain all election-related dates from your *Board of Elections*. Some might even give you current lists and daily e-mail updates for those in your precinct who request mail-in ballots. Contact the targeted voters who received mail-in ballots by phone or in person to ensure that the mail-in ballots are indeed returned. For perspective, depending on the state, mail-in ballots are sent out 45 days ahead of Election Day for the military and 20 days ahead for all others. Make sure that any like-minded elderly and disabled voters receive mail-in ballots or have transportation to a polling location. For sure, contact all targeted voters in your neighborhood precinct prior to the start of early voting.

Seventy-two hours prior to Election Day, make sure to contact all targeted voters. Follow up on Election Day with personal visits or phone calls to confirm that they have voted. Even contacting voters around 4:30 p.m. and 6:30 p.m. on Election Day can result in a difference-making vote. Each polling location will post, throughout the Election Day, lists of all those who have voted up to that point in time, including early voting and mail-in voting. You can check these postings to determine which of the targeted voters in your neighborhood precinct have already voted and who may need a gentle reminder. Check with your *Board of Elections* to determine the specific times and locations for postings at polling places.

Can Others Help Me?

To recruit others to help you with *Get-Out-The-Vote* efforts in your neighborhood precinct, you *MUST* personally *ASK* people to volunteer. Volunteers do not have to live in your precinct. Start by asking like-minded neighbors, friends, relatives, and work colleagues. Also ask like-minded members you know from church or clubs. Reach out by asking potential volunteers at social hours of local liberty-minded organization meetings or people standing in line at *limited government* oriented events. You can also use your neighborhood precinct's *Voter Registration Record* to identify potential volunteer candidates. Get contact information and provide your contact information to everyone you meet, even if someone might not be interested in volunteering at the time. They may become sufficiently frustrated at a future time and will then reach out to you to volunteer.

You will learn that volunteers who have never done anything like this before will quickly catch on and have an enjoyable experience. The easiest way to train new volunteers in *Get-Out-The-Vote* efforts is to have them join an experienced person for just one session. You will find that a number of your newly-recruited volunteers may have done *Get-Out-The-Vote* efforts in prior elections. Use these experienced volunteers to help teach the more detailed mechanics of *Get-Out-The-Vote* efforts. Experience shows that new volunteers will quickly learn the best practices and will be enthused to pursue them on their own by the third house. They usually learn that it is fun to engage like-minded voters and oftentimes they make new friends in their neighborhood. I experienced this myself when I recruited neighbors to help me with *Get-Out-The-Vote* efforts in my own precinct. After Election Day, nearly all volunteers, none of whom had ever before done door-to-door political canvassing, sent me very positive, unsolicited comments about their experience.

You can have experienced volunteers conduct role plays at meetings, showing the right way and the wrong way to do block walking or to make calls. Generally, volunteers will also teach each other through shop talk at meetings. You will find that a nonpartisan, Constitution-based, educational, door-to-door voter engagement approach to *Get-Out-The-Vote* is far less threatening and intimidating for volunteers. It is important to inform potential *Get-Out-The-Vote* volunteers that they would only be volunteering for several hours per week using a well-defined and proven method. Assure them that training will be provided and direct them to our website (http://thevoicesofamerica.org/) for self-guided instructions.

Once you start *Get-Out-The-Vote* efforts in your neighborhood precinct, you will end up recruiting even more volunteers through your current group of volunteers and from those targeted voters whom you contact. Before you know it, your *Neighborhood Meeting* group of *We the People* volunteers will become the most powerful political force within the precinct. You can get by with about five volunteers, but the ideal number of volunteers per precinct is about ten.

What To Do and Not Do?

Based on anecdotal evidence, take along a child in your neighborhood *Get-Out-The-Vote* efforts because many more doors will open. Depending on the child's age, they can even learn about civic duty from the ensuing conversations. If you do not have a child, maybe you can convince one of your neighbors to send one of their older children along. Step back from doors after knocking or ringing bells and take off sunglasses when speaking with anyone. Use your own speaking style since informal communication works best. Focus on the future versus rehashing the past, i.e., where we would like to be versus the present. Be succinct and a good listener. Be pleasant and friendly. If you do not have an answer, admit it and promise to get back to the voter. If no one is home, leave a door hanger, *Voter Guide*, or any other relevant material wedged in the door.

Do not pursue *Get-Out-The-Vote* efforts on your own. Have two people cover opposite sides of the street. Do not go into homes or apartments, even if invited. Do not walk across people's yards. Do not advocate for or endorse a specific candidate. Do not sell, argue, or antagonize. Avoid controversial issues and do not wear offensive clothing. Do not make derogatory comments about specific organizations, candidates, or officeholders, nor make statements about anyone that cannot be proven. Do not place anything in mailboxes, since this is against the law.

What Impact Will It Have?

The effectiveness of the *Get-Out-The-Vote* methodology of going door-to-door in your neighborhood prior to elections, relative to many other techniques, is best demonstrated in the following chart.

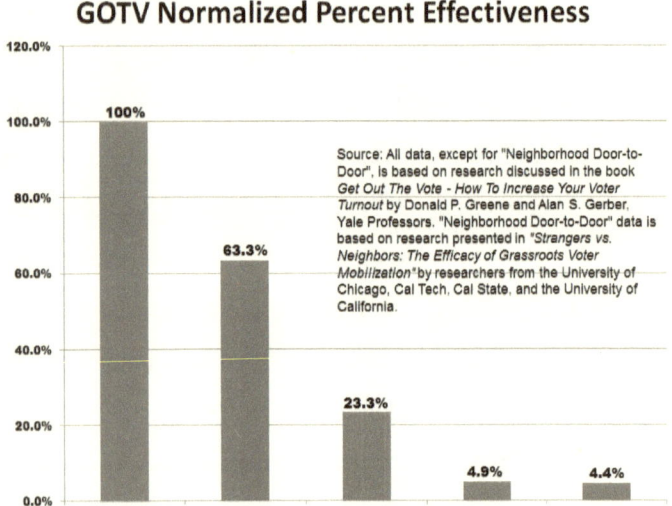

Note how going door-to-door in someone else's neighborhood drops the effectiveness from 100% to 63.3%. Also, note that it takes about twenty script-based phone calls to a given home relative to one door-to-door neighborhood visit to have the same *Get-Out-The-Vote* effect. Clearly, the ability to state, *"I am one of your concerned neighbors"* has an impact! Statistical analysis has shown that voter mobilization campaigns have enduring effects, with 33% of those mobilized for one election continuing to vote in subsequent elections.

Despite being statistically far inferior, the Republican Party tends to favor other voter mobilization techniques such as mass advertising, mass mailings, and centralized professional phone banks. Their campaign consultants feel that they can better control the message, it is easier, and the campaign consultants make more money. Campaign consultants usually make about 15% commission on the utilized capabilities in addition to their monthly consulting fees. In contrast, the Democrats, and especially those who believe in *Big Government,* have for decades understood that the secret to winning elections is through door-to-door precinct organizing. That is how they have been able to consistently win key state and federal elections with just twenty percent of registered voters who favor *Big Government.* These wins have enabled them to impact politics and policy for decades with their *Big Government* ideology.

Get-Out-The-Vote Aids

If no one is home or if the contacted voter needs more information, leave a nonpartisan door hanger or *Voter Guide* with the voter or on the door. Typically, about 50% of households will not be home on any one pass. If possible, try to return at some other time to personally talk with each of the targeted voters on your list.

Door Hangers

Nonpartisan door hangers cannot be for or against a specific party or candidate. They can include principles which are to be used as a basis for voting such as *limited government*, *free markets*, or *individual liberties*. They can also state what trends you are against such as failed stimulus spending, job-killing cap & trade laws, and government-run healthcare. Furthermore, they can provide data-based information such as a specific candidate's or party's voting record, government spending data, or polling data. Importantly, make sure the door hanger includes dates, times, and locations for *early voting* and Election Day voting. State who paid for the door hanger and include your contact information. A two-sided sample is shown on the next page.

STOP OUT-OF-CONTROL SPENDING & OVER-REGULATION OF ECONOMY

VOTE FOR CANDIDATES
who support:
LIMITED GOVERNMENT
FREE MARKETS
INDIVIDUAL LIBERTIES

TELL LIKE-MINDED
Neighbors, Friends, &
Relatives to

VOTE

Created by TheVoicesOfAmerica.org

BIG GOVERNMENT STATE OF THE UNION

ECONOMY / JOBS
- Fewest % of people working since 1983
- Highest national debt ever! +60% since '08
- High food price inflation
- Struggling housing market
- 50% increase in food-stamp recipients. Welfare's work training requirement eliminated.
- S&P first ever credit warning for U.S.

OBAMACARE *(LARGEST TAX INCREASE EVER)*
- Much higher taxes & insurance premiums
- Costs $2.6 trillion in first 10 years
- Cuts Medicare by $700 billion
- Greater bureaucracy & regulations

ENERGY POLICY
- Gas prices highest ever: > $4/gal
- "War" on oil/gas drilling and coal industry
- Blocked "Keystone Oil Pipeline"
- Billions of tax $ lost on Green Energy Projects
- EPA rules CO_2 as pollutant, overruling Senate

SELECTIVE ENFORCEMENT OF LAWS
- Attorney General found in contempt of Congress
- Unenforced Immigration laws; Intimidates states
- DOJ fights Voting Integrity laws of states
- DOJ refuses to enforce Defense of Marriage Act

INDIVIDUAL LIBERTIES
- Assault on Religious Freedom with contraception & abortion Health Care Mandates
- FCC internet controls overrule Congress & Court

EDUCATION
- Higher costs = poorer student test results
- We rank 30th in Math & 23rd in Science in world
- Teacher unions prosper, while students suffer

Voting Location on November 6
WEST CHESTER TOWNSHIP HALL - ADMIN
(TRUSTEE HALL)
9113 CINCINNATI DAYTON RD 45069
WEST CHESTER, OH

Created by TheVoicesOfAmerica.org

Voter Guides

Nonpartisan *Voter Guides* provide factual information for all candidates, such as who they are and where they stand on the issues, from the President of the United States all the way down to the school board. These *Voter Guides* can be disseminated before elections by *Neighborhood Meeting* volunteers who go door-to-door using *Get-Out-The-Vote* methodology or, inexpensively, as newspaper inserts. They can also be distributed on Election Day near polling locations.

The nonpartisan *Voter Guide* concept was successfully tested in four general elections in Ohio and has been phenomenal in what a difference it made. One of the most compelling examples of effectiveness was shared by *The Abigail Adams Project*, who led this effort in past elections. It pertains to the *Voter Guide's* effectiveness in the African-American community. In fact, *The Abigail Adams Project's Voter Guide* concept was very much influenced by this anecdotal example in which African-American voters were not at all interested in party specific, partisan *Voter Guides*, especially those from the GOP, but were very much interested in nonpartisan *Voter Guides*. In just one such interaction, two African-American women took the *Voter Guides*, studied them, and concluded that they could no longer vote for the incumbent political candidate since his voting record violated many of their closely-held principles, values, and faith-based beliefs. Net, as Thomas Jefferson stated, *"Informed voters can be trusted to vote for the right candidates"*.

The 2010 Ohio District 18 Congressional race is yet another excellent example of the power of *Voter Guides* and *Constituent Town Halls,* discussed in Chapter 11, since the incumbent candidate chose not to participate in either and consequently lost the election by over 19%. This was considered an upset and was not anticipated by the *political Establishment*. In contrast, the Constitutional Party candidate, who participated in both the *Constituent Town Halls* and the *Voter Guide*, received over twice as many votes in Ohio-18 than any other Independent Party district candidate anywhere else in Ohio, despite having spent very little on his campaign and having no campaign manager. The *Voter Guide*, which for the incumbent politician stated, *"Refused to answer questionnaire"*, was distributed to 65,000 voters in the district three days prior to the election in a Sunday newspaper insert. Using newspaper inserts is very affordable.

---

[104] Peggy Noonan, "America Is So in Play", *Wall Street Journal*, August 27, 2015.

Chapter 15

=================

Organizations to Enable and Serve

"An organization's ability to learn, and translate that learning into action rapidly, is the ultimate competitive advantage."
– Jack Welch, former CEO of General Electric

"Organizations exist to serve. Period. Leaders live to serve. Period."
- Tom Peters, management consultant and author of *Search of Excellence*

"Community organizing is all about building grassroots support. It's about identifying the people around you with whom you can create a common, passionate cause. And it's about ignoring the conventional wisdom of company politics and instead playing the game by very different rules."
- Tom Peters, management consultant and author of *Search of Excellence*

As *Neighborhood Meeting* groups grow, there may come a time when it becomes appropriate to join with other groups, either physically or virtually, to form an organization. The primary purpose for creating the organization should be to achieve economies of scale in enabling, coordinating, and executing local *Neighborhood Meeting* group strategies and tactics. We should practice what we preach regarding our *limited government* orientation in the way we create organizations, i.e., by not centralizing power and wealth. Instead, we should create organizations of "enabling servant-leaders". Local *Neighborhood Meeting* groups know best what actions are required to accomplish their goals.

As an example, an organization can use existing technological capabilities to virtually network *Neighborhood Meeting* groups' strategies and tactics across geographies. More specifically, members in each of the *Neighborhood Meeting* groups can be networked, e.g., via social media, to coordinate and collaborate on specific strategies or tactics. Individual members in geographically dispersed groups interested in pursuing the media actions described in Chapter 5, for instance, can virtually network to coordinate their talking points and share best practices, such as Letters-to-the-Editor. This can be achieved for all of the strategies and actions discussed in this book. It would achieve the desired goal for the organization as an enabler and creator of scale.

A real world example of this enabling concept occurred in 2012. Consistent with *TheVoicesOfAmerica.org's Get-Out-The-Vote* focus, I was asked by the *Ohio Liberty Coalition* to help deploy *rVotes*,[105] a *Get-Out-The-Vote* enabling software, to hundreds of *limited government* organizations throughout Ohio. I was assisted in this task by the software engineer who originally created *rVotes*, volunteers who vetted all those who would gain online access to the software, and those who volunteered to provide online *rVotes* training to all who gained access. Vetting those who would gain access to this campaign software was accomplished by personally interviewing individual leaders who requested access by phone, as well as by checking the provided references. The local leaders were then tasked with providing access locally only to trusted members of their respective organizations. All that was required for this campaign software deployment throughout Ohio was centralized funding for the software and four geographically dispersed volunteers.

To be successful, larger organizations must meet certain criteria. Foremost, if the organization is not growing, it is dying. This principle also exists for businesses and explains their constant focus on growth. The organization must be action-oriented and have tangible successes to achieve membership growth. People, especially volunteers, will only be drawn to an organization that is successful. Members should never feel that you are wasting their time.

Reaching out to other *Neighborhood Meeting* groups will help grow the organization. Or conversely, as an organization, start *Neighborhood Meeting* groups as a means to grow. Reaching out to like-minded family, friends, and acquaintances will also grow the organization. Flyers can be posted at churches, community centers, libraries, schools, or meetings of other organizations. Recruitment works best if people are asked *in person* to join the organization and their involvement appeals to their self-interest, such as personal considerations or personal values and principles. Personal considerations include concern for the future of children and grandchildren, issues of concern, companionship, or simply wanting to have fun. Values and principles can be grounded in faith, ethics, ideology, or merely wanting to do one's civic duty. Organizations must have a regular public presence in order to give them visibility and allow new people an opportunity to join. Presence can be achieved by hosting *Constituent Town*

Halls as discussed in Chapter 11, sponsoring educational events open to the public, or leading protests/marches.

Experience has shown that contacting like-minded constituents by calling them or via robocall, using targeting methods identified in the *Get-Out-The-Vote* Chapter 14, will also work. One of the *limited government* oriented organization leaders in Sandusky, Ohio did exactly this by consistently using robocalls to grow his membership. As a result, twenty or more new members frequently showed up at each of his meetings. His robocall script was similar to the following: *Hello, my name is*

_____ . *I am a concerned citizen from your neighborhood who is troubled by how politicians of both parties are bankrupting our country and are jeopardizing our children's and grandchildren's future. ... If you are concerned about what is going on in Washington, I would welcome your involvement with our community group... Together we can make a difference! ... Please call me at* _____ *or e-mail me at*

_____ . I received similar testimonials from leaders in other states who used robocalls in this fashion to grow their organizations.

To grow and engage membership, organizations will need to adopt many of the best management business practices and apply them to the volunteer effort. This is necessary for organizations to successfully recruit, inspire, and retain volunteers in order to expand an organization's effectiveness and reach. Specifically, these management practices include: recruiting volunteers, teaching them how to be an effective servant-leader, breaking "complicated" tasks into simpler tasks, and allowing capable volunteers to rapidly assume responsibility and ownership. It is best to initially allow volunteers to gravitate to the tasks that are most aligned with their passions and skills. Over time, volunteers will acquire new skills and interests, thus being able to help out more broadly. Education and information sharing can be enabled by the organization by providing online learning and social media capabilities. Members can then access these capabilities on their own time.

Importantly, the organization should be based on nonpartisan, commonly shared values and principles that are timeless and thus sustainable, not on advocating for specific people or issues. People and issues come and go and are not sustainable. This does not preclude the organization from taking positions on people and issues, but only if these positions are based on nonpartisan principles and values.

It is usually best to start an organization with a temporary steering committee and defer leadership selections for six to twelve months. Likewise, do not initially spend too much time on bylaws, etc. which are bound to drive many potential leaders and members from the organization.

Organization meetings should only occur to make decisions, not for information sharing or for education. Action-focused meetings can include further discussion and decisions on strategies and tactics, member and volunteer recruitment, or discussion and evaluation of overall organizational positions and goals. Members respond best if they have to choose between proposals versus working them up from scratch in meetings. Meetings should generally be no longer than two hours and members should receive the agenda prior to the meeting. Call members personally or via robocalls prior to meetings to maximize attendance. Be sure that microphones are available so that all attendees are able to hear the speakers. Usually this is required for groups in excess of about 30-40 members or if the room has low ceilings. Try to do something fun at every meeting. Use a meeting facilitator to insure that the meeting stays on time, make sure that all points of view are heard, bring discussions to closure, and record volunteer commitments. Be sure that meeting minutes with key decisions and commitments are shared with all members after meetings.

Remember at all times that meetings are of paramount importance and can make or break an organization!

While *limited government*, civic-oriented organizations might be tempted to establish themselves as either a 501(c)(3) or 501(c)(4) nonprofit organization, this may not be advisable due to the bookkeeping requirements, likely IRS paperwork and delays in getting approval, and the overall IRS harassment precedent of *limited government* oriented organizations. Because of these considerations, many *limited government*, civic-oriented organizations have opted to establish themselves as for-profit *Limited Liability Corporations* (LLC). The main downside is that donations will no longer be tax-deductible for those making the donations, but on the other hand, donations will be kept more private than for nonprofits. The charter should clearly state that all revenue and income will be spent on out-of-pocket expenses consistent with the organization's mission and that there will be no profit disbursements. It is advisable to consult legal and tax experts to properly establish an organization's legal entity and the associated tax consequences.

---

[105] Peter H. Wolf, *rVotes*, TheVoicesOfAmerica.org,

http://thevoicesofamerica.org/rVotes.html (November 7, 2015).

Epilogue - Call to Action

It is imperative that each one of us in the *Silent Majority* picks one or more of the strategies and tactics discussed in this book to take back our government from *elite politicians* and powerful special interests. While you may be tempted to think that it will not make a difference, the cumulative effect of all of those in the *Silent Majority* throughout our nation's neighborhoods will be immense. We must act before it is too late!

Every day we are subjected to more protests and outrage made to appear spontaneous and broad-based, but which are in fact instigated by well-trained *Community Organizers*.[106] Unseen by the *Silent Majority*, thousands of *Community Organizers* operate within our midst throughout the nation and coordinate their actions with *Big Government* advocates.[107] Their protests and outrage are broadly covered and shared through a complicit *Big Government* oriented media and through social media in an attempt to legitimize the issue and pressure politicians and those in power to yield to their demands. All of their demands are focused on obtaining even more concessions from the *Silent Majority* and giving more power to the centralized *Big Government* as an enforcer of these concessions. Throughout history, oppressive *Big Governments* have used citizen collaborators and agitators to secure absolute power over the majority of its citizens, e.g., Mussolini's black shirts, Hitler's brown shirts, China's Red Guard, and goon squads in Venezuela and Cuba. Now we are literally witnessing this situation in our own country.

As further evidence of this collusion and collaboration, the U.S. Executive Branch is funding these *Community Organizing* organizations, such as *Organizing for Action, La Raza, AmeriCorps,* and *My Brother's Keeper*, by funneling millions of legal settlement dollars to them. Specifically, in settlement agreements with corporate bad actors the Department of Justice mandates that some of the penalty money be paid in the form of "donations" to these *Community Organizing* nonprofits. The Department of Justice is currently in the process of funneling more than half-a-billion dollars to these activist groups.[108] All of this is occurring despite the Department of Justice's own internal guidelines that discourage such donations. The *Community Organizing* organizations need this money to pay for organizer salaries which can be as high as $40,000/year with benefits.[109]

In light of these developments, it is imperative that we learn from *Community Organizers* by replicating their organizing methods through *Neighborhood Meeting* groups and pursue the strategies and tactics discussed in each of this book's chapters to counter their actions. At minimum, do not allow yourself to be silenced anymore by *Political Correctness,* ignore the faux protests, and beware of biased news reporting. Speak up with truth and logic. The *Silent Majority* has many more people than those who are incited by *Community Organizers*, but the *Silent Majority* must become passionate and motivated to act in order for *American Exceptionalism* to prevail!

---

[106] Matthew Vadum, *OBAMA'S PERMANENT PROTEST - Why the rise in rioting and civil unrest under Obama is no coincidence, but part of the plan*, Frontpage Magazine, http://www.frontpagemag.com/fpm/260841/obamas-permanent-protest-matthew-vadum (November 19, 2015).

[107] Sara Rimer, *Community Organizing Never Looked So Good*, New York Times, http://www.nytimes.com/2009/04/12/fashion/12organizer.html (April 10, 2009).

---

[108] Kimberly A. Strassel, *Justice's Liberal Slush Fund - Legal settlements are being used to funnel millions to left-wing activists like La Raza*, Wall Street Journal, http://www.wsj.com/articles/justices-liberal-slush-fund-1449188273, (December 3, 2015).

[109] http://www.nytimes.com/2009/04/12/fashion/ 12organizer.html

Sources

Adam Fergusson, *When Money Dies: The Nightmare of Deficit Spending, Devaluation, and Hyperinflation in Weimar Germany*, (New York: Perseus Books Group, 2010).

Alexis de Tocqueville, *Democracy in America* (New York: Signet Classics – Penguin Group, 2000).

Arthur C. Brooks, *The Conservative Heart: How to Build a Fairer, Happier, and More Prosperous America* (New York: Broadside Press, HarperCollins Publishers, 2015).

Betsy Myers, *Take the Lead: Motivate, Inspire, and Bring Out the Best in Yourself and Everyone Around You*, Reprint Edition (New York: Atria Books - Simon & Schuster, 2012).

Dale Franks, *Slackernomics: Basic Economics for People Who Think Economics is Boring* (Bloomington, IN: iUniverse, 2004).

Daniel Hannan, *The New Road to Serfdom: A Letter of Warning to America*, Reprint Edition (New York: Broadside Books – HarperCollins, 2011).

Donald P. Green, Alan S. Gerber, *Get Out the Vote: How to Increase Voter Turnout*, 2nd Edition (Washington: Brookings Institution Press, 2008).

F. A. Hayek, *The Reader's Digest condensed version of 'The Road to Serfdom'. Now includes 'The Intellectuals and Socialism'*, http://www.iea.org.uk/publications/research/the-road-to-serfdom (July 19, 2005).

Father Leslie J. Walker, ed., *The Discourses of Niccolo Machiavelli* (London: Routledge, 2013).

Friedrich A. Hayek, Bruce Caldwell, ed., *The Road to Serfdom: Text and Documents--The Definitive Edition, The Collected Works of F. A. Hayek,* Volume 2 (Chicago: University of Chicago Press, 2007).

Gene Sharp, *From Dictatorship to Democracy: A Conceptual Framework for Liberation* (New York: The New Press, 2012).

George Orwell, Christopher Hitchens, ed., *Animal Farm and 1984* (Boston: Houghton Mifflin Harcourt, 2003).

Jim Hayes, ed., *The Original Reagan Conservative: Ronald Reagan's Conservative Ideas In His Own Words* (Seattle: CreateSpace Independent Publishing Platform – Amazon, 2008).

Joost A. M. Meerloo, *The Rape of the Mind: The Psychology of Thought Control, Menticide, and Brainwashing* (San Diego, CA: Progressive Press, 2009).

Kristen Wolf, *NOW HEAR THIS - THE NINE LAWS OF SUCCESSFUL ADVOCACY COMMUNICATIONS*, Fenton Communications, http://www.beyondpesticides.org/assets/media/documents/how-to/media/Packard_Brochure.pdf (November 7, 2015).

Marshall Ganz, *Organizing: People, Power and Change*, John F. Kennedy School of Government Harvard University, https://annastarrrose.files.wordpress.com/2011/06/ganz-course-notes.pdf (Spring, 2008).

Marshall Ganz, *Organizing: People, Power and Change*, John F. Kennedy School of Government Harvard University, http://isites.harvard.edu/fs/docs/icb.topic113119.files/8_3.pdf (Fall, 2006).

Max & Kendall Bobo, *Organizing for Social Change*, 4th Edition (Santa Ana, CA: The Forum Press, 2010).

Naftali Bendavid, *The Thumpin': How Rahm Emanuel and the Democrats Learned to Be Ruthless and Ended the Republican Revolution* (New York: Doubleday, 2007).

Richard John Neuhaus, *The Naked Public Square: Religion and Democracy in America*, 2nd Edition (Grand Rapids, MI: Wm. B. Eerdmans Publishing Co, 1988).

Rob Witwer, *The Blueprint: How the Democrats Won Colorado (and Why Republicans Everywhere Should Care)* (Golden, CO: Fulcrum Publishing Inc, 2010).

Robert A. Heinlein, *Take Back Your Government!: A Practical Handbook for the Private Citizen Who Wants Democracy to Work* (Wake Forest, NC: Baen books, 1992).

Saul D. Alinsky, *Rules for Radicals: A Practical Primer for Realistic Radicals* (New York: Vintage Books, 1989).

Scott W. Rasmussen, *In Search of Self-Governance* (Charleston: CreateSpace, 2010).

Sinclair Lewis, Michael Meyer, ed., *It Can't Happen Here*, Reprint edition (New York: Berkley Publishing Group /NAL Trade, 2005).

Thomas E. Woods Jr., *The Church and the Market: A Catholic Defense of the Free Economy* (Lenham, Maryland: Lexington Books, 2005).

Timothy Daughtry, Gary Casselman, *Waking the Sleeping Giant: How Mainstream Americans Can Beat Liberals at Their Own Game* (New York: Beaufort Books, 2012).

Timothy E. Cook, *Governing with the News: The News Media as a Political Institution* (Chicago: University of Chicago Press, 1954).

W. Cleon Skousen, *The 5000 Year Leap* (Malta, ID: National Center for Constitutional Studies, 2007).

About the Author

Peter H. Wolf co-founded *TheVoicesOfAmerica.org* in 2009 with the goal of providing *Get-Out-The-Vote* best practices nationally to help liberty-minded individuals and organizations gain increased political clout and win elections. He traveled the country giving presentations to thousands of individuals and leaders. One of his keynote convention talks streamed live on *C-SPAN*. He retired from a top *Fortune 50* corporation after a successful career in research & development and supply chain redesign. Considered a key *Fortune 50* e-commerce supply chain thought leader, he was quoted in both *The Wall Street Journal* and *Chemical Week*.